MW01051272

MAKE A GIFT FOR BABY

Reworked and adapted for
American needleworkers by

CARTER HOUCK

E. P. DUTTON   NEW YORK

First published, 1986, in the United States by E. P. Dutton.

Copyright © 1981 by Ondorisha Publishers, Ltd.
First published in Japan by Ondorisha Publishers, Ltd.

All rights reserved.

No part of this book may be reproduced or transmitted in any form
or by any means, electronic or mechanical, including photocopy,
recording, or any storage and retrieval system now known or to be
invented, without permission in writing from the publishers, except
by a reviewer who wishes to quote brief passages in connection with
a review written for inclusion in a magazine, newspaper, or
broadcast.

Published simultaneously in Canada by Fitzhenry & Whiteside
Limited, Toronto.

CUSA

Published in the United States by E. P. Dutton, a division of New
American Library, 2 Park Avenue, New York, N.Y. 10016.

Library of Congress Catalog Card Number: 85-70221
ISBN: 0-525-24292-9 (cloth)
ISBN: 0-525-48140-0 (paper)

Printed and bound in Japan.

10 9 8 7 6 5 4 3 2 1
First Edition

BABY'S OUTFIT

STRIPED DRESS #1 AND WHITE SHOES #2

Directions: Dress (#1)—p. 2; Shoes (#2)—p. 69

1. Draw patterns full size from scaled diagrams (see p. 107). Add ½ in. seam allowance to all edges of all pieces except:

Lay-on-fold lines of A, C, E, and F.

Neck edges of A and B.

Add 1 in. hem to lower edges of E and F.

2. Follow pattern layout, pin and cut fabric by pattern pieces. Cut two 7 ins. strips of 1¼-in. bias for cuff binding.

3. Mark all folded centers, and *center* and *fold* lines on B and D, with a clip at ends.

4. Run gathering threads, as marked, on skirt pieces C and D, and sleeve G.

5. Gather C and seam to A, gather D pieces to B. Topstitch waistline, Fig. a.

6. Turn back edges on *fold lines* and hem above *leave open* mark. Sew on snaps, Fig. b. Seam D pieces closed below marks. Seam F to lower edge of D and E to C.

7. Gather and bind lower sleeve edge. Seam underarm to complete sleeves, Fig. c.

8. Gather upper edges of sleeves and seam into armholes. Topstitch if desired, Fig. d.

9. Hem ends of eyelet, gather to fit neck. Bind neck and eyelet together, Fig. e.

10. Crochet belt loops at sides and front, Fig. f.

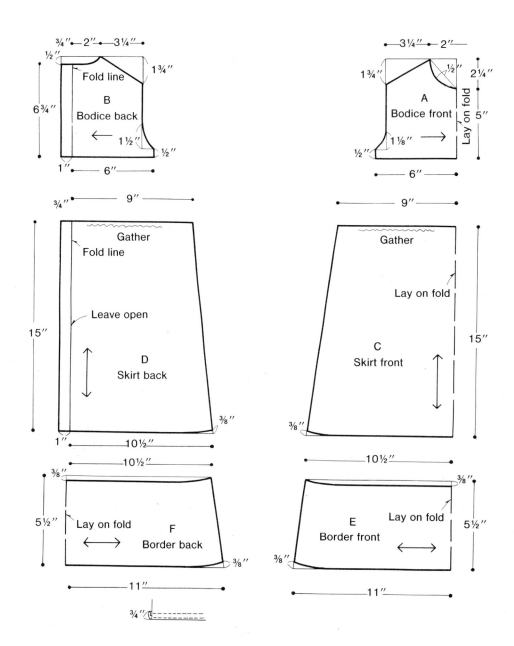

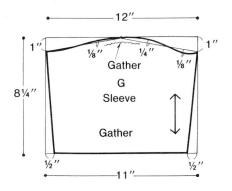

12″

1″   1″

⅛″   ¼″

⅛″

Gather

G

Sleeve

8¼″

Gather

½″   ½″

11″

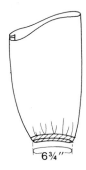

6¾″

Fig. c

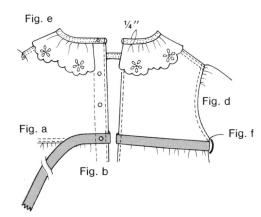

Fig. e

¼″

Fig. d

Fig. a

Fig. f

Fig. b

Fig. f

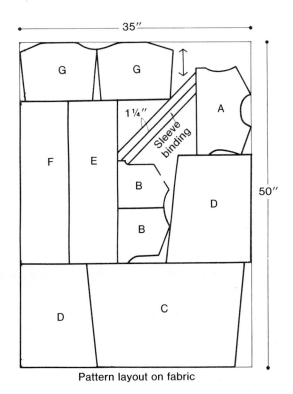

35″

G   G

1¼″

Sleeve binding

A

F   E

B

50″

D

B

D   C

Pattern layout on fabric

Materials:
(Fabrics 36 to 45 ins. wide)

Striped cotton fabric	1½ yds.
White bias binding	12 ins.
White eyelet edging (2 ins.)	½ yds.
Washable satin ribbon (1 in.)	1½ yds.
Snap fasteners (small)	6
Pink embroidery thread	Small amount

BABY'S PINK BUBBLE DRESS #3
AND MATCHING BAG #4
Directions: Dress (#3)—pp. 6–7; Bag (#4)—pp. 7, 72–73

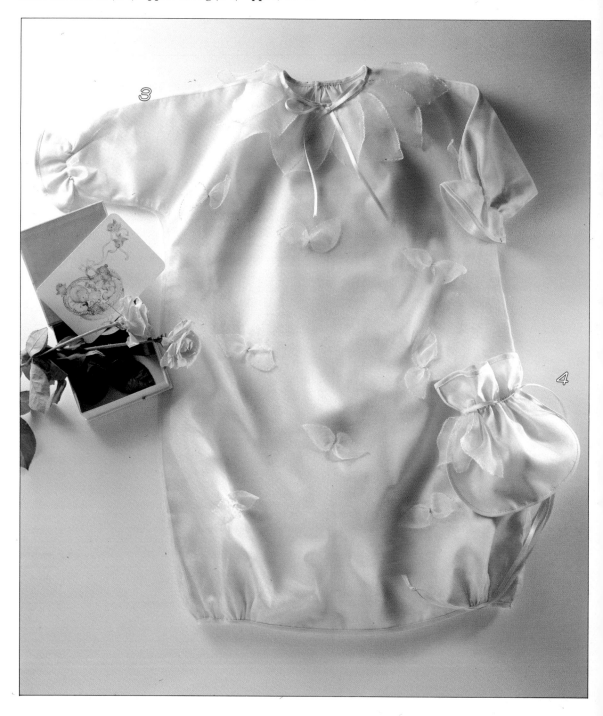

BABY'S LONG COAT DRESS #5
AND BONNET #6
Directions: Dress (#5)—pp. 70–71; Bonnet (#6)—p. 72.

4

5

1. Draw patterns full size from scaled diagrams (see p. 107). Add ½ in. seam allowance to all edges of all pieces except:

Lay-on-fold of A and B.

Neck, sleeve ends, and lower edge of A and B.

2. Lay A and B on length-grain fold of organdy and lining and cut. Cut nine decorative petals and sixteen neck-edge petals from organdy.

3. Mark centers by clipping ends of folds.

4. Seam front to back at shoulders and side seams. Repeat on lining. Clip seams at underarm curve and press all seams open flat.

5. Pin lining inside dress, wrong sides together, matching seam lines. Gather neck to 11 or 12 ins.

6. Split center back from neck down 4½ ins. Bind dress and lining together, making a small miter at bottom of split, Fig. a.

7. Finish edges of petals with zigzag stitches. Overlap them about ½ in. and gather to fit neck. Bind neck and petals together, Fig. b. Attach snap.

8. Make a casing around each sleeve with two rows of topstitching, ½ in. apart and 1¼ ins. from lower edge. Run 6 ins. of elastic in each. Bind sleeve ends, Fig. c.

9. Gather lower edge of dress and lining together to 30 ins. and bind, Fig. d.

10. Finish decorative petals with zigzag stitches. With embroidery thread gather center of each and stitch to dress, Fig. e.

Materials: for dress only
(Fabrics 36 to 45 ins. wide)

Pink organdy	1 ½ yds.
Pink cotton lining	1 ½ yds.
Pink bias binding (½ in.)	1 ¾ yds.
Pink satin ribbon (¼ in.)	1 yd.
Soft elastic (¼ in.)	⅜ yd.
Snap fasteners (small)	1
Pink embroidery thread	Small amount

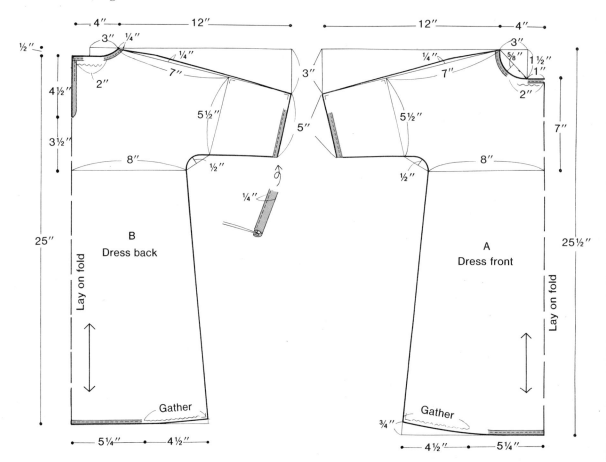

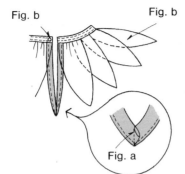

Fig. b   Fig. b

Fig. a

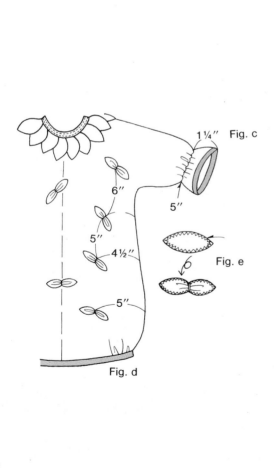

1¼″   Fig. c

5″

6″

5″

4½″   Fig. e

5″

5″

Fig. d

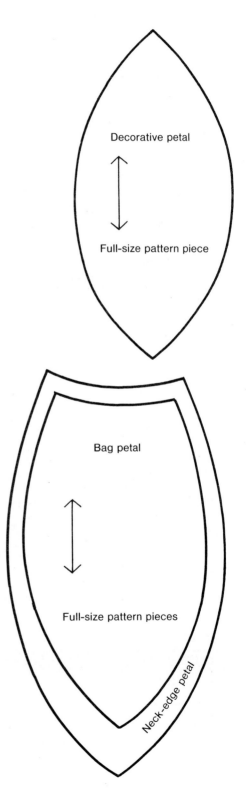

Decorative petal

Full-size pattern piece

Bag petal

Full-size pattern pieces

Neck-edge petal

BONNETS
WHITE WITH DEEP RUFFLE #7
WHITE WITH SMALL RUFFLE #8　　BLUE #9

Directions: Bonnet (#7)—p. 73; Bonnet (#8)—p. 73; Bonnet (#9)—p. 74

WHITE BABY DRESS #10
AND PANTIES #11

Directions: Dress (#10)—p. 11; Panties (#11)—p. 10

1. Draw patterns full size from scaled diagrams (see p. 107). Add ½-in. seam allowance to all edges of all pieces except:

Lay-on-fold of A, B, C, G, and E.

Add 1-in. hem to upper edges of A and B.

2. Follow arrows and fold lines to lay patterns on fabric and cut.

3. Mark all folded centers, and *fold* and *center* lines of D and F, with a clip at ends.

4. Cut X eyelet into 20-in. and 40-in. pieces. Gather shorter piece to upper line on B and stitch in place. Seam A to B along sides and crotch. Gather longer eyelet to lower line on A and B, stitch in place.

5. Turn 1-in. hem on upper edge of panties, turn under ¼ in., and stitch to make casing for ½-in. elastic, Fig. a.

6. Seam ungathered pieces of Y around each leg opening. Seam bias binding on same line, turn to inside and stitch along other edge to make casing for ¼-in. elastic, Fig. b.

7. Make ¹⁄₁₆-in. pin tucks in C (taking up a total of ⅛ in. per tuck), Fig. c.

8. Seam E to F along sides, press and make pin tucks all around. Gather 66 ins. of Y and X, stitch in top tuck and hem, Fig. d.

9. Seam C to D along shoulders. Gather 22 ins. of Y to fit 14 ins. of Z, join. Miter corners, Fig. e 1, and ease eyelet to fit back of neck, Fig. e 2. Turn neck edge ¼ in. toward right side and stitch both edges of Z in place.

10. Seam 16 ins. of Y to outer edge of G. Cut 16 ins. of X, taper ends, Fig. f.

11. Gather X and G-Y together to fit armhole, seam in place, Fig. g.

12. Gather E-F and seam *wrong sides together* to C-D. Cover seam with Y and run ribbon, Fig. h. Run ribbon around neck.

13. Finish back opening as on striped dress (pp. 2–3), Fig. b.

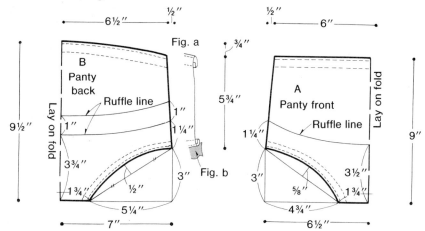

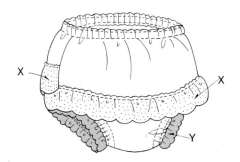

Materials: (Fabrics 36 to 45 ins. wide)	Dress	Panties
Soft white cotton	¾ yd.	⅜ yd.
White eyelet edging (X) (1 ¼ ins.)	2 ½ yds.	1 ¾ yds.
White eyelet edging (Y) (¾ in.)	2 ½ yds.	¾ yd.
White eyelet beading* (Z) (¾ in.)	1 ¼ yds.	
Pink satin ribbon (¼ in.)	2 yds.	
Soft elastic (¼ in.)		½ yd.
Soft elastic (½ in.)		½ yd.
White bias binding (½ in.)		¾ yd.
Snap fasteners (small)	6	

* Beading: Eyelet or lace with slots for threading ribbon.

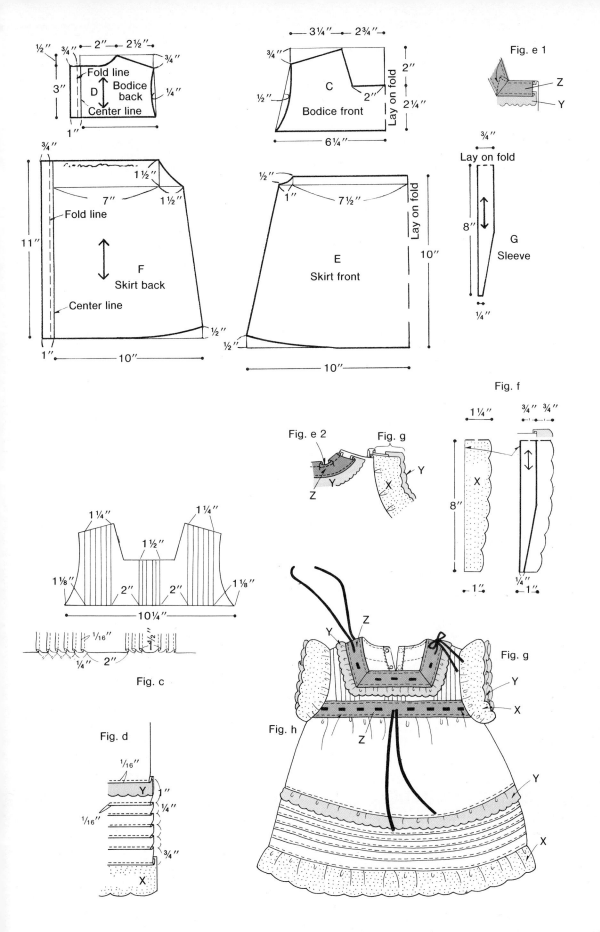

½″ ¾″ ← 2″ → ← 2½″ →
Fold line
¾″
¾″
3″ Bodice
back ¼″
D
Center line
1″

← 3¼″ → ← 2¾″ →
¾″
½″
C 2″
Bodice front Lay on fold 2″
2¼″
← 6¼″ →

Fig. e 1
Z
Y

¾″
¾″
Fold line
1½″
7″ 1½″
Fold line
Lay on fold
½″
1″
7½″
Lay on fold
11″
E
Skirt front
10″
F
Skirt back
Center line
½″
1″ ← 10″ →
½″
← 10″ →

¾″
Lay on fold
8″
G
Sleeve
¼″

Fig. f
1¼″ ¾″ ¾″
8″ X X
1″ ¼″ 1″

Fig. e 2 Fig. g
Y X
Z

1¼″ 1½″ 1¼″
1⅛″ 2″ 2″ 1⅛″
← 10¼″ →

1/16″ 1½″ 1″
¼″ 2″
Fig. c

Fig. d
1/16″
Y 1″
¼″
1/16″
¾″
X

Z
Y Z
Fig. g
Y
X
Fig. h
Z
Y
X

BIBS

LARGE TIE-ON #12   HEART-SHAPED BIB #13

Directions: Bib (#12)—p. 75; Bib (#13)— p. 75.

BIBS

TIE-ON BIB #14   ROUND BIB #15   SQUARE BIB #16

Directions: Tie-on Bib (#14)—p. 78; Round Bib
(#15)—pp. 15 and 89; Square Bib (#16)—p. 14

1. Draw patterns full size from scaled diagrams (see p.107). Add ½-in. seam allowance to all edges of all pieces except:

　Lay-on-fold lines of A and C.
　Neck edges of all pieces.

2. Lay A and C on length-grain fold, B on double fabric. Cut A and B from main fabric. Cut B and C from lining fabric.

3. Mark centers by clipping ends of folds.

4. Cut and gather 12 ins. of eyelet to fit across front, Fig. a.

5. Make tuck as marked on front, incorporating eyelet, Fig. b.

6. Fold 36 ins. of binding and stitch, Fig. c.

7. Cut 2-in. piece of stitched binding and make button loop at back, Fig. d.

8. Embroider flowers, as shown, on outer layer.

9. Seam backs and fronts together at shoulders. Gather a 14-in. piece of eyelet to fit lower edge and two 20-in. pieces to go over shoulders. Cut remainder of stitched bias into four even pieces. Incorporate bias and eyelet between bib and lining, as the two are seamed together around the edge. Turn right side out through neck, Fig. e.

10. Cut 30 ins. of binding to bind neck, leaving ties, Fig. f.

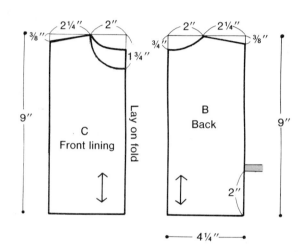

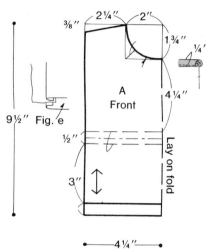

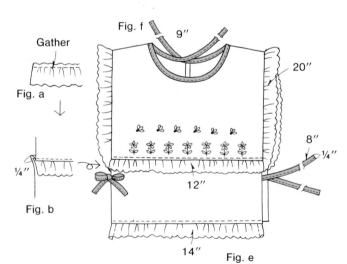

Materials:
(Fabrics 36 to 45 ins. wide)

White cotton fabric	⅜ yd.
White lining fabric	⅜ yd.
White eyelet edging (1 in.)	2 yds.
White bias binding (½ in.)	1¾ yds.
Six-strand embroidery floss in yellow, green, dark and light blue, less than 1 skein each.	
Small white button	

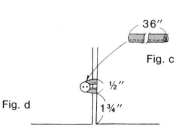

Lazy Daisy and French Knots
(See p. 110)

French Knot
(See p. 110)

Lazy Daisy
(See p. 110)

Embroidery pattern

⑮ ROUND BIB   shown on p. 13

1. Trace pattern from page 89. Add ½-in. seam allowance except on:
    Neck edge.
2. Cut on fold twice.
3. Gather lace to fit outer edge.
4. Embroider flowers, as shown, on outer layer.
5. Seam two layers together with lace between, turn right side out, Fig. a.
6. Bind neck edge, leaving tie ends, Fig. b.

Full-size pattern on p. 89

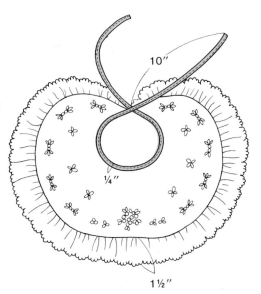

Materials:
(Fabrics 36 to 45 ins. wide)

White cotton fabric	¼ yd.
White eyelet edging (1 ½ in.)	1⅜ yds.
White bias binding (½ in.)	⅞ yd.
Six-strand embroidery floss in yellow-green, light and dark pink, light and dark blue, less than 1 skein each.	

Continued on page 89

VEST AND MITTENS
VEST #17   MITTENS #18, #19, #20

Directions: Vest (#17)—p. 83; Mittens (#18)—pp. 81–82;
Mittens (#19)—pp. 81–82; Mittens (#20)—pp. 81–82

JACKET #21 AND PANTIES #22

Directions: Jacket (#21)—pp. 18–19;   Panties (#22)—pp. 18–19

21 22 JACKET AND PANTIES shown on p.17

1. Draw patterns full size from scaled diagram (see p.107). Add ½-in. seam allowance to all edges of all pieces except:
Lay-on-fold lines of B and D
Neck edges of A and B
Add 1⅛-in. hems to ends of panties.
2. Seam A to B along shoulders and sides, Fig. a.
3. Gather 1¾ yds. of 1-in. eyelet edging to fit around jacket edge. Seam to edge along with bias binding, Fig. b.
4. Embroider flowers, as shown, on jacket front.
5. Gather two 14-in. pieces of 1-in. eyelet to fit lower edges of sleeves, complete as on jacket edge, Fig. b.
6. Gather remaining 1-in. eyelet to fit neck. Bind neck and eyelet together, leaving 10-in. ties, Fig. c.
7. Run 6 ins. of elastic through each sleeve binding and seam underarm of sleeves.
8. Ease sleeves to armholes, seam in place, and finish with binding, Fig. d.
9. Turn 1⅛-in. hems on each end of panties, turn under ¼ in. and stitch to make casing for ¼-in. elastic, as shown, Fig. e.
10. Finish the legs with slightly gathered ⅝-in. eyelet and bias binding, Fig. b.
11. Run 9 ins. of elastic through the bias around each leg, and 9 ins. each across front and back of panties at waist, pinning each end to secure until side seams are stitched, Fig. f.

Materials:
(Fabrics 36 to 45 ins. wide)

	Jacket	Panties
Cream cotton jersey	⅝ yd. for both	
Eyelet edging (1 in.)	3½ yds.	
Eyelet edging (⅝ in.)		¾ yd.
Cream bias binding (½ in.)	3 yds.	1 yd.
Elastic (¼ in.)	⅓ yd.	½ yd.
Six-strand embroidery floss in white, yellow, and green, less than 1 skein each.		

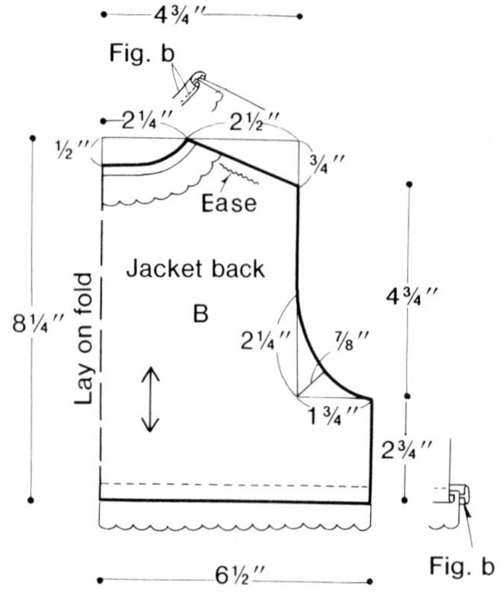

4¾″
Fig. b
2¼″
2½″
½″
¾″
Ease
Jacket back
B
Lay on fold
8¼″
4¾″
2¼″
⅞″
1¾″
2¾″
6½″
Fig. b

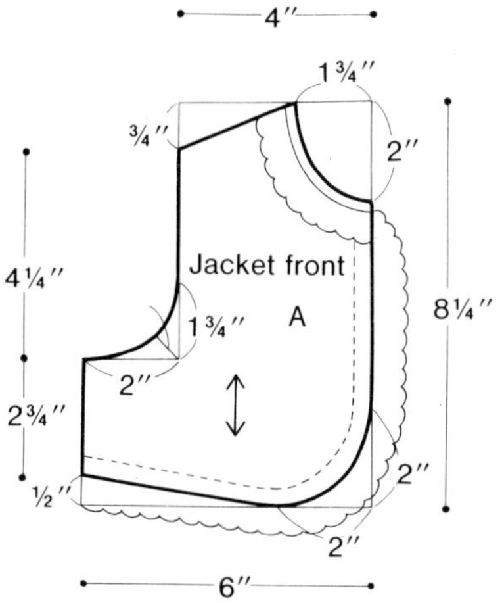

4″
1¾″
¾″
2″
4¼″
Jacket front
A
1¾″
8¼″
2″
2¾″
½″
2″
2″
6″

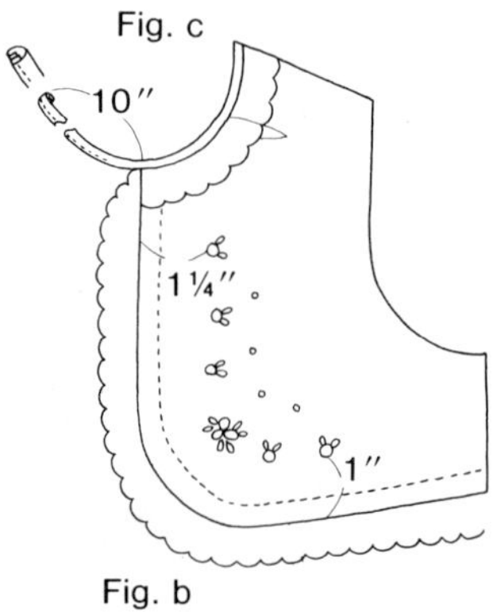

Fig. c
10″
1¼″
1″
Fig. b

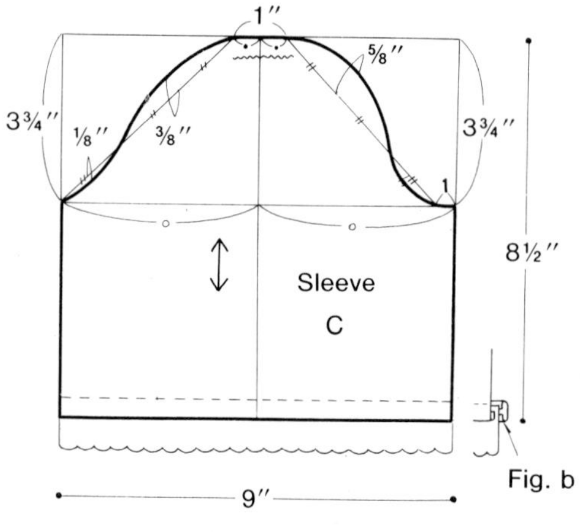

1″
⅝″
3¾″
⅛″
⅜″
3¾″
1
Sleeve
C
8½″
9″
Fig. b

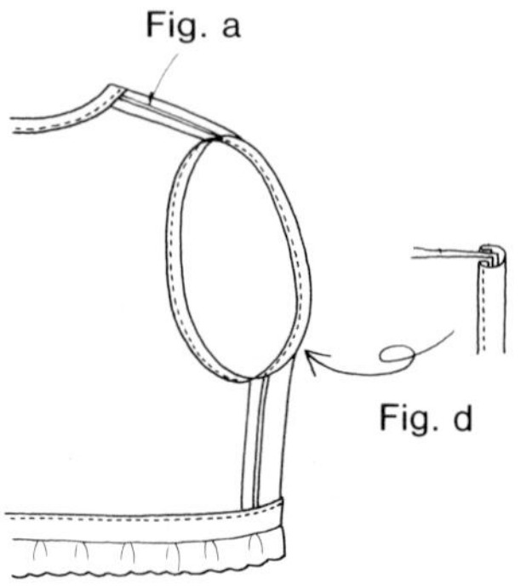

Fig. a
Fig. d

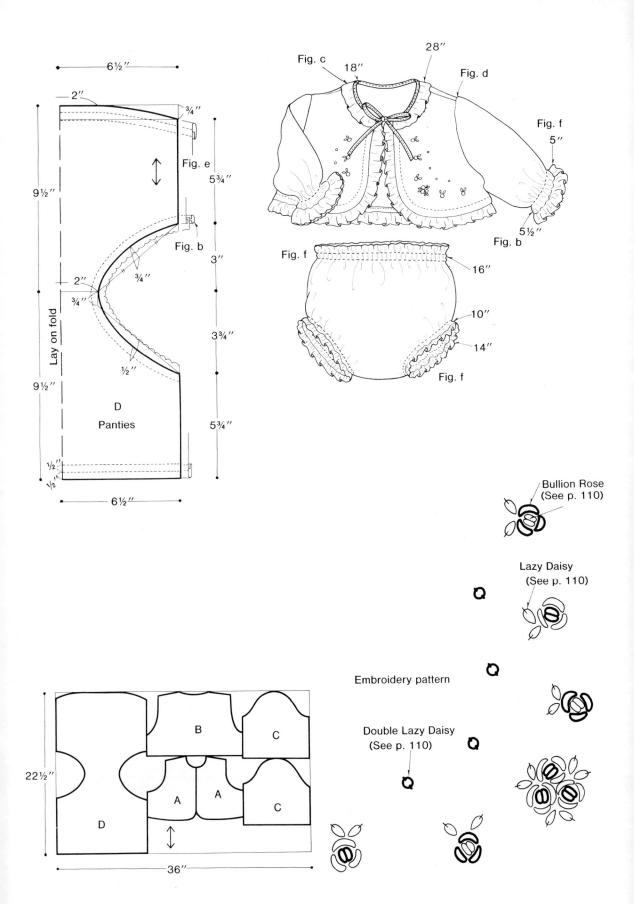

6½″

2″

¾″

9½″

Fig. e

5¾″

Lay on fold

Fig. b

2″

¾″

¾″

3″

½″

3¾″

D
Panties

½″

½″

5¾″

9½″

6½″

Fig. c

18″

28″

Fig. d

Fig. f
5″

Fig. b

5½″

Fig. b

Fig. f

16″

10″

14″

Fig. f

Bullion Rose
(See p. 110)

Lazy Daisy
(See p. 110)

Embroidery pattern

Double Lazy Daisy
(See p. 110)

22½″

B

C

A

A

C

D

36″

25

23

24

26

27

28

Directions: Booties (#23)—p. 80; Booties (#24)—p. 80;
Booties (#25)—p. 22; Booties (#26)—p. 22;
Booties (#27)—p. 22; Booties (#28)—p. 22;

BOOTIES

White Tyrolean Felt #23 and Blue Tyrolean Felt #24
White Eyelet #25 and Lavender Terry #26
White Satin #27 and Pink Quilted #28   White Embroidered Cotton #29
and Blue Embroidered Cotton #30   Flowered Flannel #31 and Pink Embroidered Flannel #32
Small Gingham Check #33 and Medium Gingham Check #34

1. Trace patterns from page 22. Add ¼-in. seam allowance to back and front of uppers only.
2. Cut four uppers and two soles from main fabric for each pair of booties.
3. For #27 only, cut same from lining, and insoles from batting.
4. Seam two uppers together along front and back for each bootie, Fig. a.
5. For #28 lay binding over seams and stitch, Fig. b.
6. For #27 seam linings same as outside.
7. Lay linings of #27 wrong side together with booties. On soles lay insoles between outside fabric and lining. Baste or stitch all edges to hold.
8. Cut ribbon into four pieces, stitch in place, Fig. c.
9. Bind upper edge of each bootie, Fig. d.
10. Bind uppers and soles together, Fig. e.

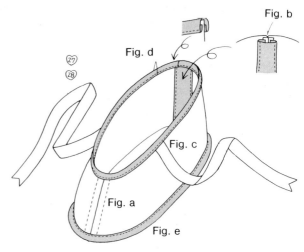

Materials:	#27	#28
Top	White satin, 12 x 8 ins.	Cotton quilt 12 x 8 ins.
Lining	White cotton, 12 x 8 ins.	
Batting	6 x 6 ins.	
Ribbon (⅝ in.)	White satin, ¾ yd.	Pink grosgrain, ¾ yd.
Bias binding (½ in.)	White, 1¾ yds.	Pink, 2 yds.

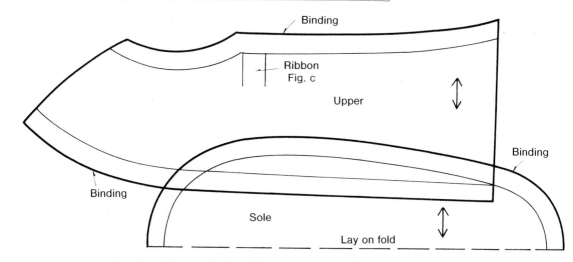

㉕㉖ RUFFLED BOOTIES
WHITE EYELET #25 AND LAVENDER TERRY #26

shown on p. 20

1. Trace patterns from page 23. Add ¼-in. seam allowance to all edges except folds.
2. Cut four uppers and two soles in main fabric for each pair, repeat in lining for #25, soles only in lining for #26.
3. For each bootie and for lining of #25 seam two uppers together along front and back, Fig. a.
4. For #26 only, topstitch seams to one side, Fig. b.
5. For #25 only, gather two 4½-in. pieces of eyelet edging into round flowers, Fig. c.

6. For #25 cut remaining edging in half and seam around top between booties and linings, Fig. d.
7. Repeat for #26, finishing with binding, Fig. e.
8. Seam uppers to soles, with lining included.
9. For #25 only, bind seam, Fig. f.
10. For #26 only, pinch seam edge on outside and stitch to form ridge, Fig. g.
11. Cut elastic in half and stitch around inside of each bootie, stretching to fit, Fig. h.
12. Sew ribbon bows on front of #26, Fig. j.

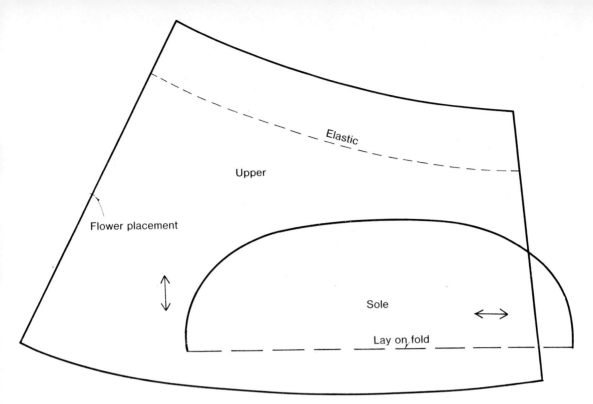

Elastic

Upper

Flower placement

Sole

Lay on fold

Materials:	#25	#26
Tops	White eyelet, 12 x 16 ins.	Lavender terry, 12 x 16 ins.
Lining	White cotton, 12 x 16 ins.	Lavender cotton, 12 x 16 ins.
Eyelet edging (¾ in.)	White, ⅞ yd.	White, ¾ yd.
Bias binding (½ in.)	White, ¾ yd.	Lavender, ½ yd.
Elastic (⅛ in.)	¼ yd.	¼ yd.
Ribbon (½ in.)		Lavender, ½ yd.

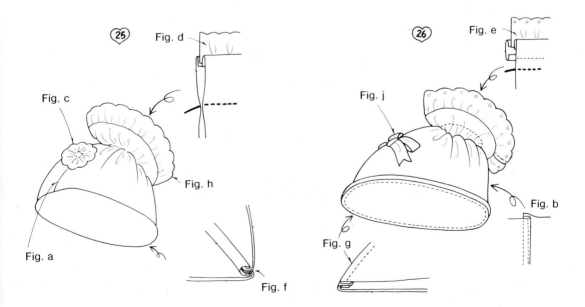

25

Fig. d

Fig. c

Fig. h

Fig. a

Fig. f

26

Fig. e

Fig. j

Fig. b

Fig. g

35

BASSINET, BASKET, AND PILLOW

37

36

1. Draw patterns full size from scaled diagrams (see p.107). Add ½-in. seam or hem allowance to all pieces to be cut from fabric (not eyelet), except: Add 1-in. hem to upper edges of ruffles.

2. For bassinet cut A, B, and two C pieces from white background fabric. Cut C from batting.

3. Cut two of each ruffle piece from blue background fabric.

4. Narrowly hem one long edge of each ruffle, Fig. a.

5. Turn other long edge under 1 in. (no turned edge as for other hem) and stitch, Fig. b.

6. Cut both widths of eyelet into four sections each, two 30 ins. and two 78 ins.

7. Gather eyelets to match ruffle strips.

8. Center wide eyelet along ruffle strip, equidistant from top and bottom. Stitch in place (zigzag stitching will prevent fraying), Fig. c.

Materials:
(Fabrics 36 to 45 ins. wide)

	Bassinet	Basket	Pillow
Blue dot white cotton	1½ yds.	¼ yd.	⅜ yd.
White dot blue cotton	1 yd.	⅛ yd.	⅜ yd.
White eyelet edging (3 ins.)	6 yds.		
White eyelet edging (2 ins.)	6 yds.	1½ yds.	2½ yds.
Blue grosgrain (¾ in.)	5 yds.	1½ yds.	1½ yds.
Batting	½ x ¾ yd.		
Polyester fiberfill			1 bag

Note: The sizes given are based on baskets currently available. It may be necessary to custom-fit any antique basket or other available sizes.

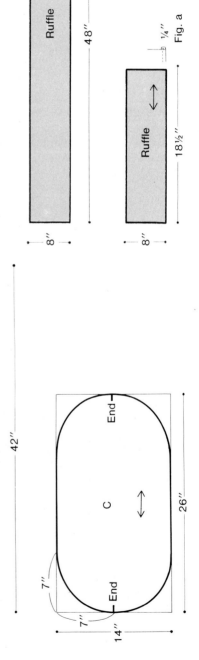

Fig. f

Fig. a

Fig. a

9. Stitch narrow eyelet along upper hemline, Fig. d.

10. Gather short sections of ruffle to 11 ins., long sections to 30 ins. Narrowly hem ends, Fig. e.

11. Seam ends of piece A to piece B, Fig. f.

12. Narrowly hem four 4-in. spaces on A-B, Fig. g.

13. Cut ribbon into two 1¼-yd. pieces and two ¾-yd. pieces. Stitch ribbon over raw upper edge of narrow eyelet on ruffle, Fig. h.

14. Turn upper unhemmed edges of A-B pieces toward wrong side and stitch upper edge of ribbon through all layers from opening to opening, Fig. j.

15. Match end marks of A-B with end marks of C, right sides of fabric together, ease sides as necessary and seam together.

16. Lay batting on bottom. Turn edges of second C piece to match and slip-stitch in place as lining over batting, Fig. k.

17. Slip the liner into basket (right side of fabric showing), ruffle out over edge, and tie ribbon ends around handles, Fig. l.

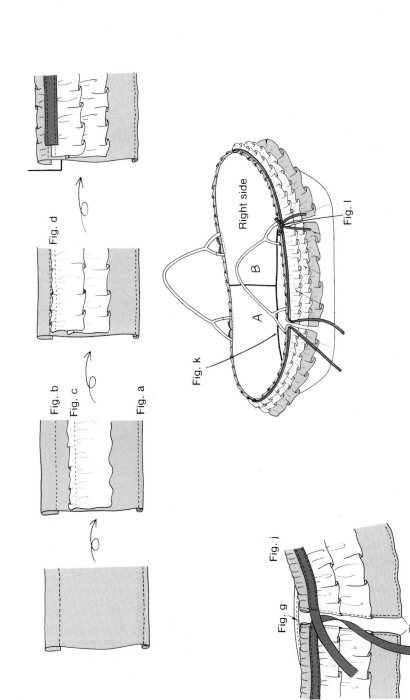

Fig. a

Fig. b

Fig. c

Fig. d

Fig. e

Fig. g

Fig. h

Fig. j

Fig. k

Right side

A

B

Fig. l

BASSINET BLANKET
AND KEEP-CLEAN BORDER
BORDER #38 AND BLANKET #39

Directions: Border—p. 30; Blanket—pp. 31, 102–103

COMFORTER
OR BLANKET COVER #40

Directions: Comforter—pp. 90–93

1. Cut white fabric to size suggested. Add ½-in. seam and hem allowance all around.

2. Sew double-edge eyelet about 1 in. from lower edge, Fig. a.

3. Narrowly hem ends and upper edge, Fig. b.

4. Gather eyelet edging to fit lower edge and seam in place, Fig. c.

5. Topstitch or zigzag to prevent raveling, Fig. d.

6. Cut squirrel from peach felt or velour and moon from yellow. Buttonhole or zigzag in place.

7. Embroider other designs, filling solid spaces with seed stitch.

8. Border may be basted or snapped to upper edge of blanket for easy removal and washing.

Materials:
(Fabrics 36 to 45 ins. wide)

White cotton	½ yd.
Double-edge eyelet (¾ in.)	1 yd.
Eyelet edging (1½ ins.)	1½ yds.
Washable felt or velour scraps	Yellow and peach
Six-strand embroidery floss, less than 1 skein each	Gold, gray, green, pink, purple, blue, yellow, and aqua

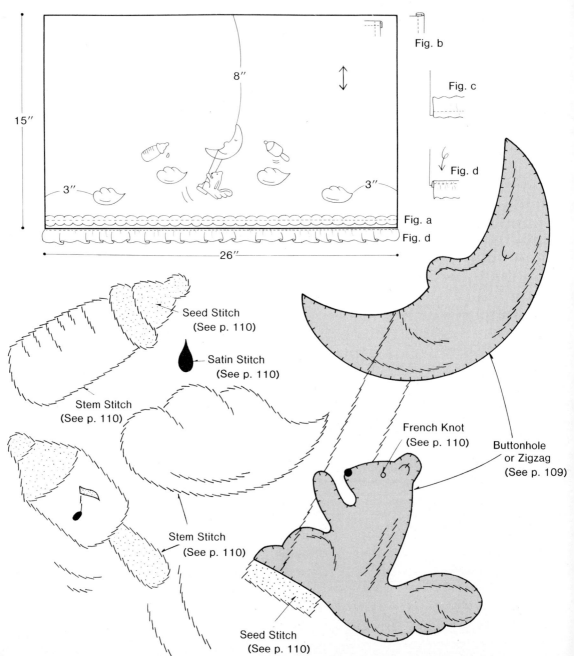

Fig. b

Fig. c

Fig. d

Fig. a
Fig. d

15″

8″

3″   3″

26″

Seed Stitch
(See p. 110)

Satin Stitch
(See p. 110)

Stem Stitch
(See p. 110)

French Knot
(See p. 110)

Buttonhole
or Zigzag
(See p. 109)

Stem Stitch
(See p. 110)

Seed Stitch
(See p. 110)

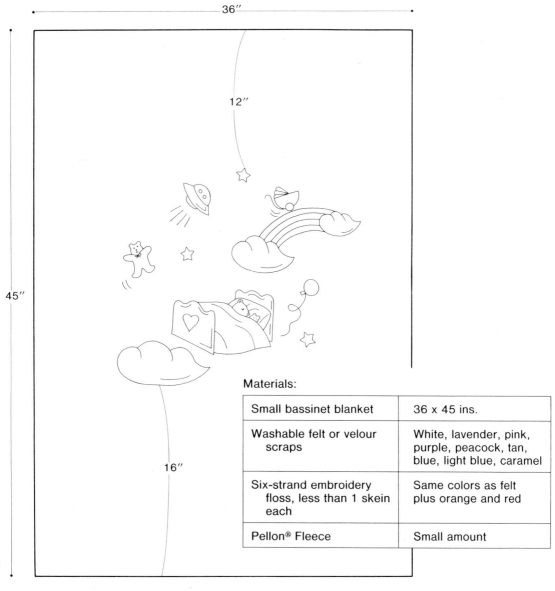

Materials:

Small bassinet blanket	36 x 45 ins.
Washable felt or velour scraps	White, lavender, pink, purple, peacock, tan, blue, light blue, caramel
Six-strand embroidery floss, less than 1 skein each	Same colors as felt plus orange and red
Pellon® Fleece	Small amount

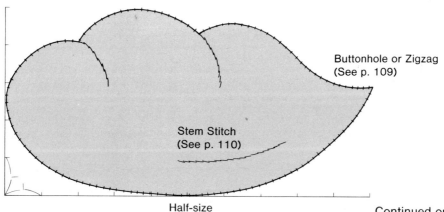

Buttonhole or Zigzag (See p. 109)

Stem Stitch (See p. 110)

Half-size

Continued on page 102

BUNTING
PINK #41 AND BLUE #42

Directions: Bunting—pp. 96–97

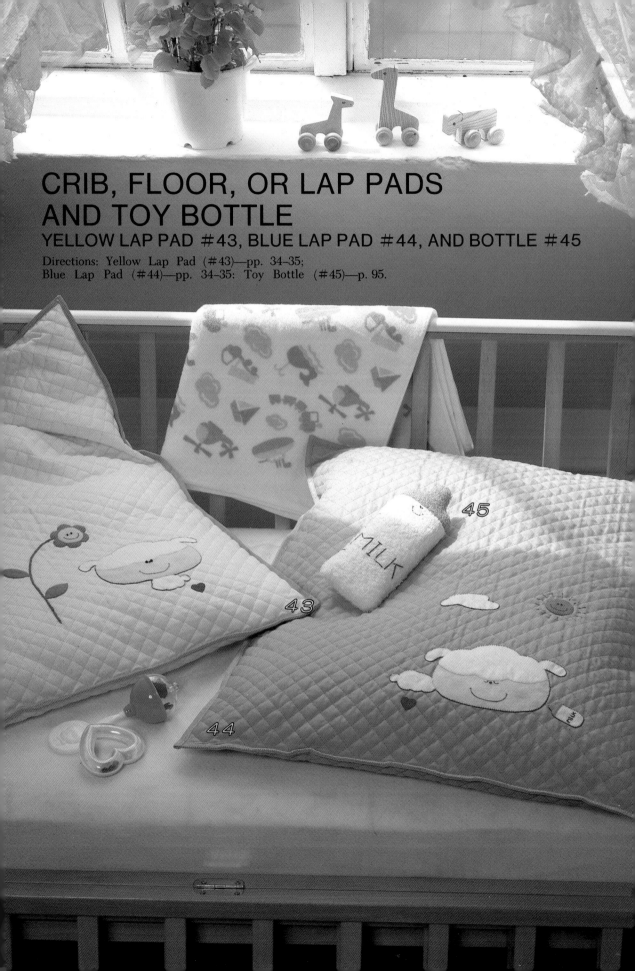

CRIB, FLOOR, OR LAP PADS AND TOY BOTTLE

YELLOW LAP PAD #43, BLUE LAP PAD #44, AND BOTTLE #45

Directions: Yellow Lap Pad (#43)—pp. 34–35;
Blue Lap Pad (#44)—pp. 34–35: Toy Bottle (#45)—p. 95.

shown on p. 33

1. Cut one piece of quilted cotton 22 x 28 ins., and two pieces 22 x 15 ins., for each pad.
2. Cut four layers Pellon® 22 x 28 ins., for each pad.
3. Bind one 22-in. edge of each smaller piece of quilted fabric. Sew dot fastenings in place, Fig. a.
4. Cut appliqué pieces from scrap, place as

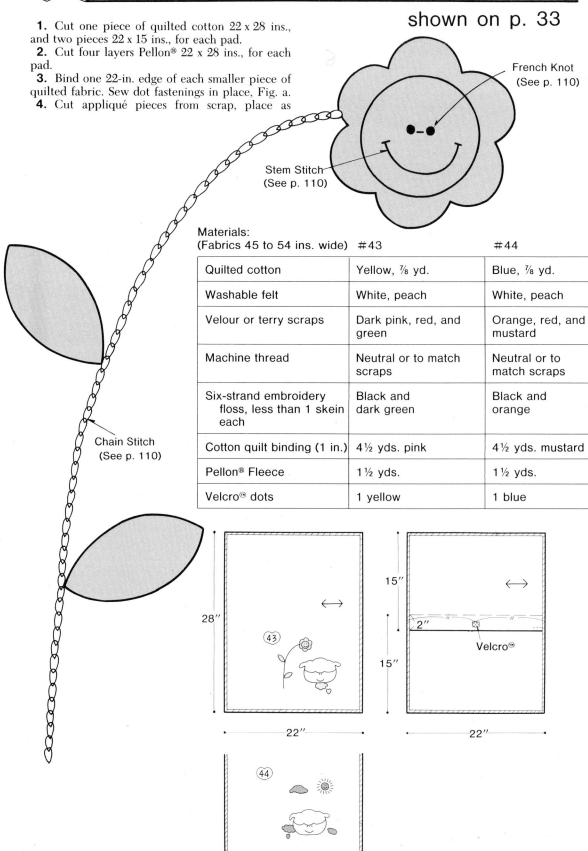

French Knot
(See p. 110)

Stem Stitch
(See p. 110)

Chain Stitch
(See p. 110)

Materials:
(Fabrics 45 to 54 ins. wide)

	#43	#44
Quilted cotton	Yellow, ⅞ yd.	Blue, ⅞ yd.
Washable felt	White, peach	White, peach
Velour or terry scraps	Dark pink, red, and green	Orange, red, and mustard
Machine thread	Neutral or to match scraps	Neutral or to match scraps
Six-strand embroidery floss, less than 1 skein each	Black and dark green	Black and orange
Cotton quilt binding (1 in.)	4½ yds. pink	4½ yds. mustard
Pellon® Fleece	1½ yds.	1½ yds.
Velcro® dots	1 yellow	1 blue

28″

22″

15″

2″

Velcro®

15″

22″

(43)

(44)

shown on larger quilted pieces, zigzag in place, and finish with touches of embroidery.

5. Lay larger piece, wrong sides together, with joined smaller pieces, stitch edges, and bind, Fig. b.

6. Stitch four layers of Pellon® Fleece together and insert through back opening.

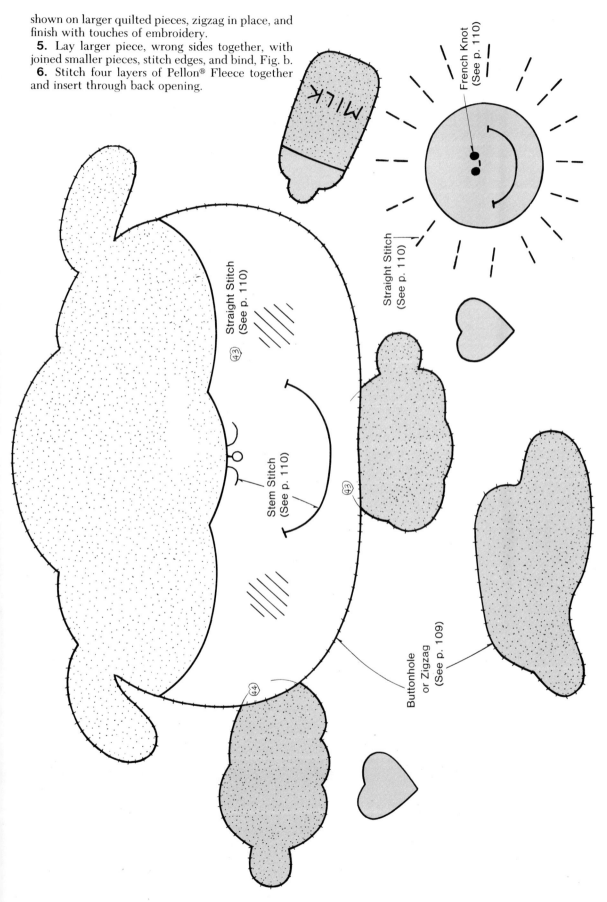

French Knot
(See p. 110)

MILK

Straight Stitch
(See p. 110)

Straight Stitch
(See p. 110)

Stem Stitch
(See p. 110)

43

43

44

Buttonhole
or Zigzag
(See p. 109)

SMALL CARRY-BAGS
PINK BAG #46 AND PINK BAG #47
WHITE BAG #48 AND WHITE BAG #49

46

47

Directions: Bags (#46 and #47)—pp. 38–39; Bags (#48 and #49)—p. 38

1. Cut batiste to 2½ x 12½ ins. Turn both edges ¼ in., as shown, and stitch ¼-in. ribbon across in Vs, for #48, Fig. a.

2. Layer all eyelet and fabric strips for both bags and stitch to form complete piece, Fig. b.

3. Seam sides, Fig. c.

4. Stitch across last row of eyelet at bottom, Fig. d.

5. Run ribbon through beading.

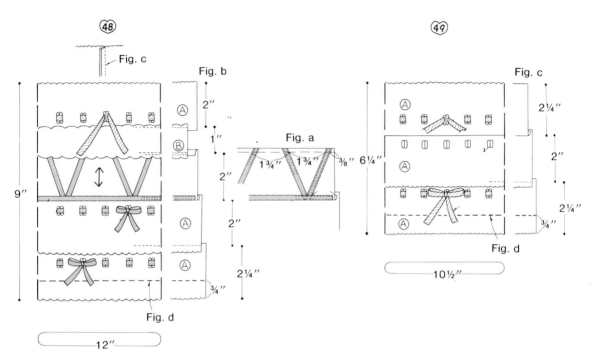

Materials:	#48	#49
White cotton batiste	14 x 4 ins.	
Eyelet edging (A) with beading* (2½ to 3 ins.)	1¼ yds.	1 yd.
Double-edge eyelet (B) (1½ ins.)	½ yd.	
Blue satin ribbon (½ in.)	½ yd.	1 yd.
Blue satin ribbon (¼ in.)	1¾ yd.	

* Beading: Eyelet or lace with slots for threading ribbon.

(46)(47) PINK BAGS　　　shown on p. 36

1. Draw patterns full size for white bags and pink overlay from diagrams (see p. 107). Add ¼-in. seam allowances to all edges of all pieces, except: Top of white main piece for #46.

2. Turn ¼-in. allowance under on pink overlay pieces and stitch in place. Stitch beads in place.

3. Work Baby and bows with embroidery floss.

4. Seam sides and bottom of bags, Fig. a.

5. Stitch eyelet beading around #46, bind top with straight pink fabric, Fig. b.

6. Turn upper edge of #47 once toward right side. Lay eyelet beading on edge and stitch.

7. Thread ribbon through eyelet beading.

Materials:	#46	#47
White cotton batiste	14 x 12 ins.	8 x 10 ins.
Pink cotton batiste	14 x 10 ins.	10 x 6 ins.
Double-edge eyelet beading* (1½ ins.)	14 ins.	10 ins.
Pink satin ribbon (¼ in.)	⅝ yd.	½ yd.
Pink beads or tiny buttons	70	60
Six-strand embroidery floss, less than 1 skein each	Pink and light pink for both bags	

* Beading: Eyelet or lace with slots for threading ribbon.

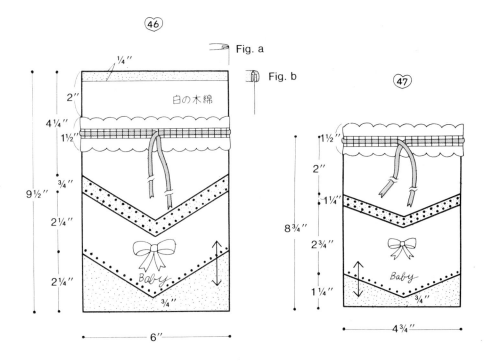

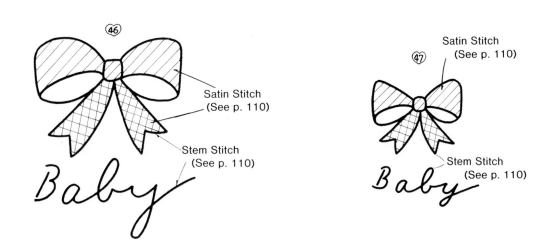

51

50

DISH COVERS
RABBITS #50 AND ANGELS #51
Directions: Rabbits (#50)—p. 43; Angels (#51)—p. 42

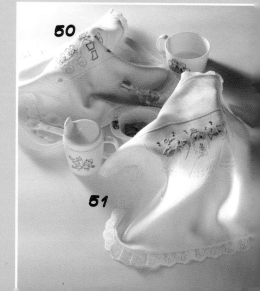

50

51

BABY BOTTLE COVERS
PINK #52 AND BLUE #53
Directions: Baby Bottle Covers, #52 and #53—p. 98

1. Embroider the chosen design, framing it with the rectangle or stem stitch (see p. 43), in the center of fabric square (see p. 42).

2. Trim square to 14½ ins., with rounded corners, Fig. a.

3. Gather eyelet to fit edge, Fig. b.

4. Overlap and blindstitch raw ends of eyelet, Fig. c.

5. Lay gathered eyelet, right sides together, with edge of linen square. Seam binding over it, Fig. d.

6. Finish binding to wrong side of linen by hand, Fig. e.

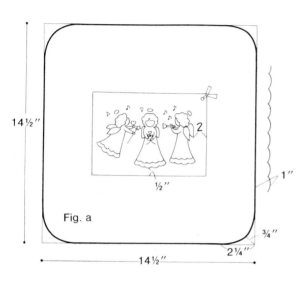

14½"

½"

1"

¾"

2¼"

14½"

Fig. a

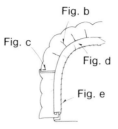

Fig. b

Fig. c

Fig. d

Fig. e

Materials:	For each cover
White linen or cotton	18 x 18 ins.
White eyelet edging (1¼ ins.)	3 yds.
White bias binding (½ in.)	1⅝ yds.
Six-strand embroidery floss, less than 1 skein each	White, yellow, blue, pink, light green, medium brown, and tan

Stem Stitch (See p. 110)

Chain Stitch (See p. 110)

Straight Stitch (See p. 110)

Satin Stitch (See p. 110)

Satin Stitch

French Knot (See p. 110)

Stem Stitch (See p. 110)

Straight Stitch (See p. 110)

Satin Stitch (See p. 110)

Chain Stitch (See p. 110)

Chain stitch

42

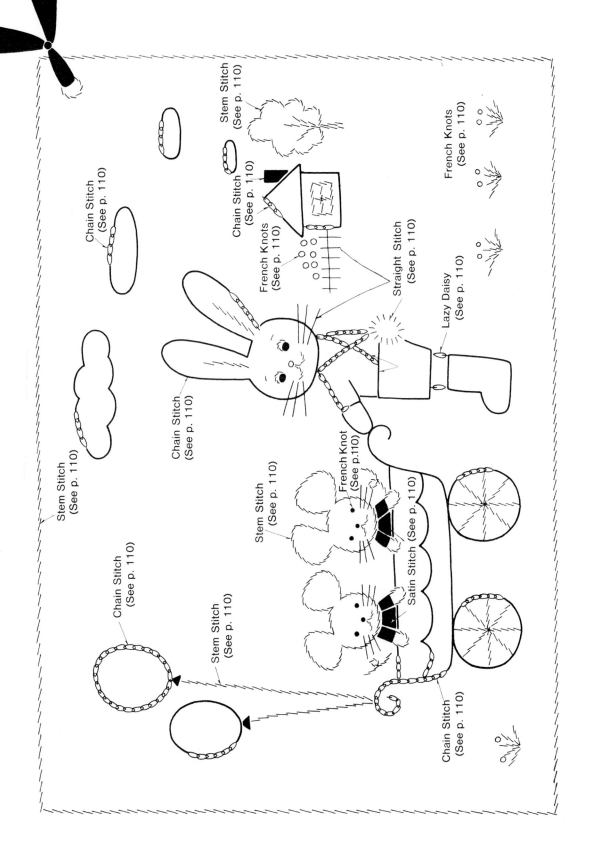

Stem Stitch (See p. 110)

Chain Stitch (See p. 110)

Chain Stitch (See p. 110)

French Knots (See p. 110)

Chain Stitch (See p. 110)

French Knots (See p. 110)

Straight Stitch (See p. 110)

Lazy Daisy (See p. 110)

French Knots (See p. 110)

Chain Stitch (See p. 110)

Stem Stitch (See p. 110)

French Knot (See p.110)

Stem Stitch (See p. 110)

Satin Stitch (See p. 110)

Chain Stitch (See p. 110)

Stem Stitch (See p. 110)

Chain Stitch (See p. 110)

BIBS AND COVERALLS

54

55

44

COVERALLS #54 AND #55
AND BIBS #56 AND #57

Directions: Bibs (#56 & 57)—pp. 46–47;
Coveralls (#54 & 55)—p. 99

56

57

1. Trace patterns from pages 46–47. Do not add seam allowance.

2. Cut 62 ins. of 1-in. wide bias strips (see p. 45) for binding each bib. Cut appliqué pieces.

3. Cut main pieces of bibs in vinyl, using pattern.

4. Work appliqué with machine zigzag. (Use tissue paper under and over vinyl if machine does not stitch smoothly.)

5. Bind edges, Fig. a, mitering corners, Fig. b.

6. Sew Velcro® in place on shoulders, Fig. c.

Materials:	#56	#57
Clear vinyl	12 x 18 ins.	
White vinyl fabric		12 x 18 ins.
Appliqué fabric	Yellow-check gingham scraps	Red polka-dot and green-check gingham scraps
Velcro®	1 ½ ins. white	1 ½ ins. white

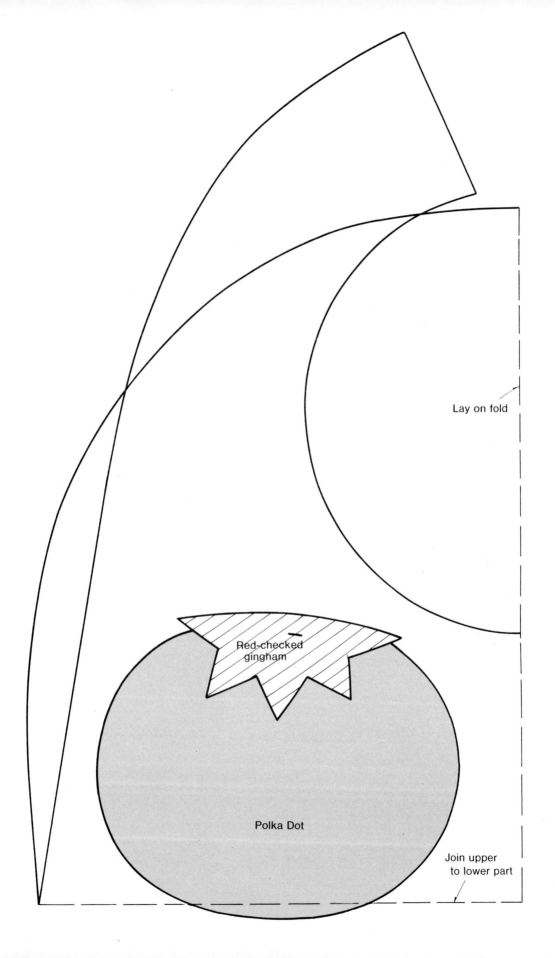

Lay on fold

Red-checked gingham

Polka Dot

Join upper to lower part

58

59

Directions: Man in the Moon (#58)—p. 50;
Elephant (#59)—p. 50; Lovely Baby (#60)—p. 50

58

60

59

EMBROIDERIES FOR
PURCHASED SHIRTS
MAN IN THE MOON #58, ELEPHANT #59,
LOVELY BABY #60

EMBROIDERIES FOR PURCHASED BIBS
AIRPLANE #61, HEART #62, CHERRIES #63

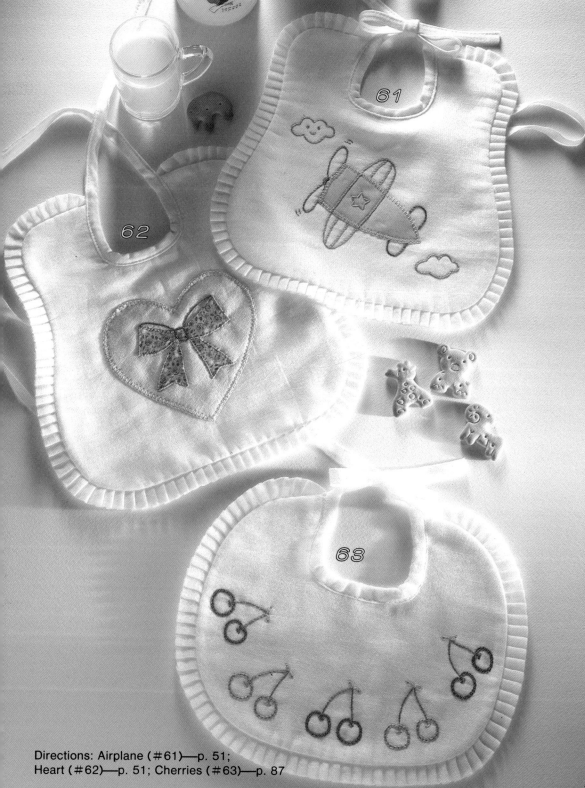

Directions: Airplane (#61)—p. 51;
Heart (#62)—p. 51; Cherries (#63)—p. 87

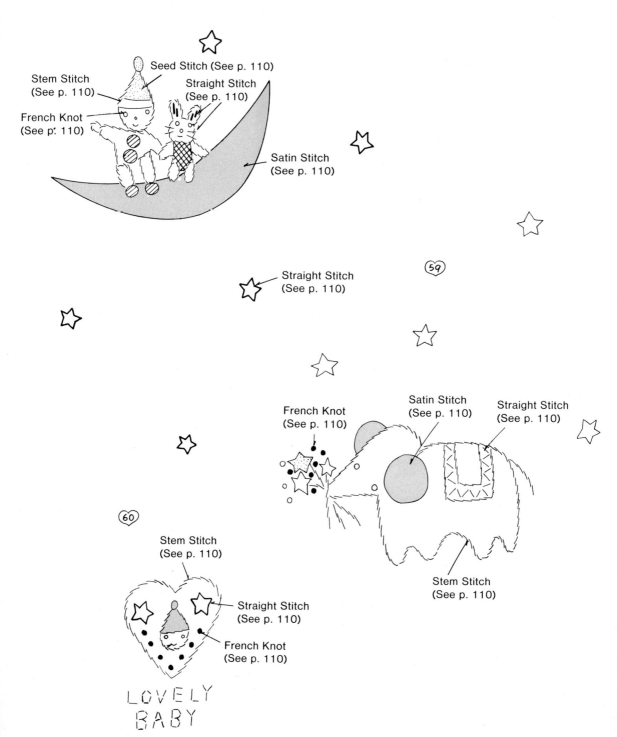

Seed Stitch (See p. 110)

Stem Stitch (See p. 110)

Straight Stitch (See p. 110)

French Knot (See p. 110)

Satin Stitch (See p. 110)

Straight Stitch (See p. 110)

59

French Knot (See p. 110)

Satin Stitch (See p. 110)

Straight Stitch (See p. 110)

60

Stem Stitch (See p. 110)

Stem Stitch (See p. 110)

Straight Stitch (See p. 110)

French Knot (See p. 110)

LOVELY BABY

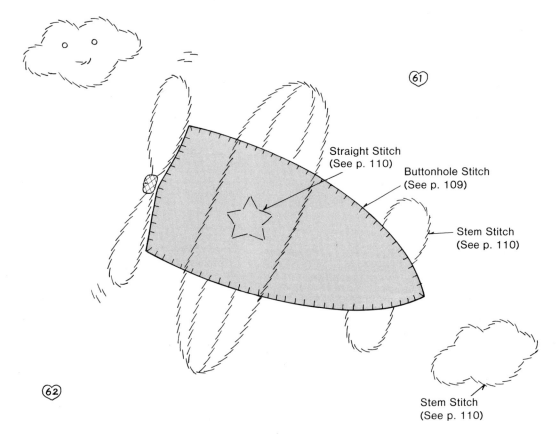

(61)

Straight Stitch
(See p. 110)

Buttonhole Stitch
(See p. 109)

Stem Stitch
(See p. 110)

(62)

Stem Stitch
(See p. 110)

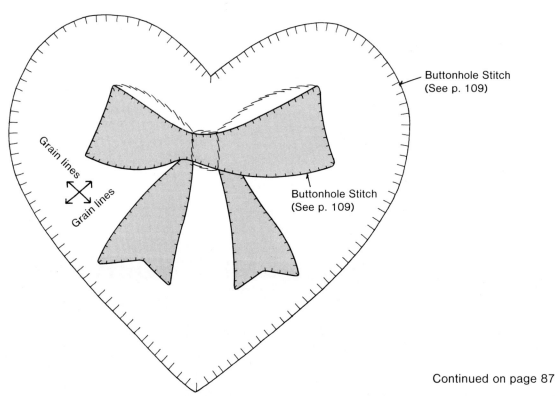

Buttonhole Stitch
(See p. 109)

Grain lines

Grain lines

Buttonhole Stitch
(See p. 109)

Continued on page 87

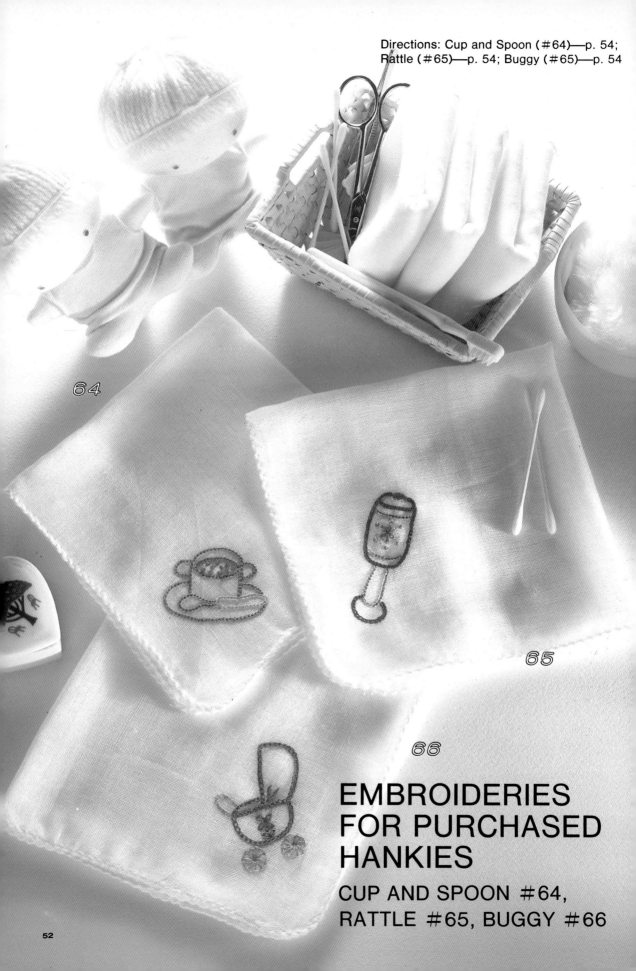

Directions: Cup and Spoon (#64)—p. 54;
Rattle (#65)—p. 54; Buggy (#65)—p. 54

64

65

66

EMBROIDERIES FOR PURCHASED HANKIES

CUP AND SPOON #64, RATTLE #65, BUGGY #66

EMBROIDERIES FOR PURCHASED SOCKS OR BOOTIES AND MITTENS

67

68

69

70

AIRPLANE #67, BIRD #68, SHIP #69, FLOWERS #70

Directions: Airplane (#67)—p. 55; Bird (#68)—p. 55;
Ship (#69)—p. 55; Flowers (#70)—p. 55

These small embroidery designs may be used on ready-made items or in any way you wish. Use the suggested stitches or any other you choose from page 110. Use six-strand embroidery floss, testing to see how many strands you want to use at any one time. Because the designs are very small, you may find that one or two strands work best.

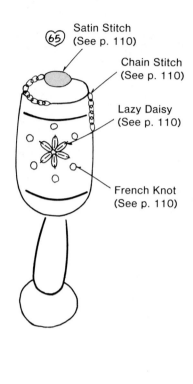

65 Satin Stitch (See p. 110)

Chain Stitch (See p. 110)

Lazy Daisy (See p. 110)

French Knot (See p. 110)

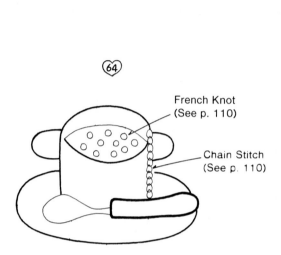

64

French Knot (See p. 110)

Chain Stitch (See p. 110)

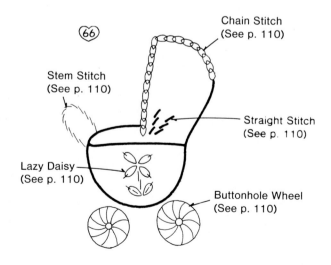

66

Chain Stitch (See p. 110)

Stem Stitch (See p. 110)

Straight Stitch (See p. 110)

Lazy Daisy (See p. 110)

Buttonhole Wheel (See p. 110)

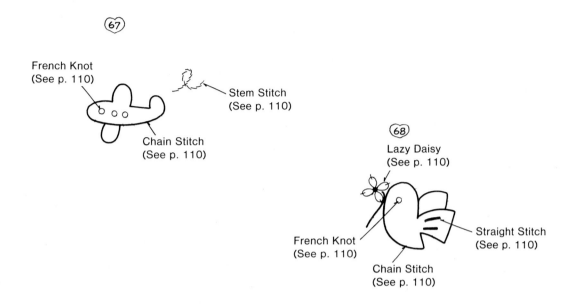

67

French Knot
(See p. 110)

Stem Stitch
(See p. 110)

Chain Stitch
(See p. 110)

68

Lazy Daisy
(See p. 110)

French Knot
(See p. 110)

Straight Stitch
(See p. 110)

Chain Stitch
(See p. 110)

69 70 Shown on purchased socks or booties, page 53

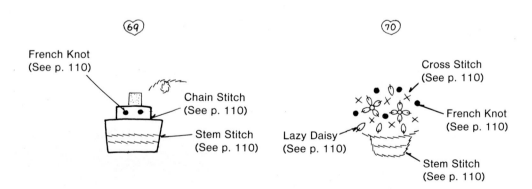

69

French Knot
(See p. 110)

Chain Stitch
(See p. 110)

Stem Stitch
(See p. 110)

70

Cross Stitch
(See p. 110)

French Knot
(See p. 110)

Lazy Daisy
(See p. 110)

Stem Stitch
(See p. 110)

TERRY WASHCLOTH BIBS

TEDDY BEAR #71, COUNTING CHERRIES #72
GREEN #74, PINK #75, BLUE #76

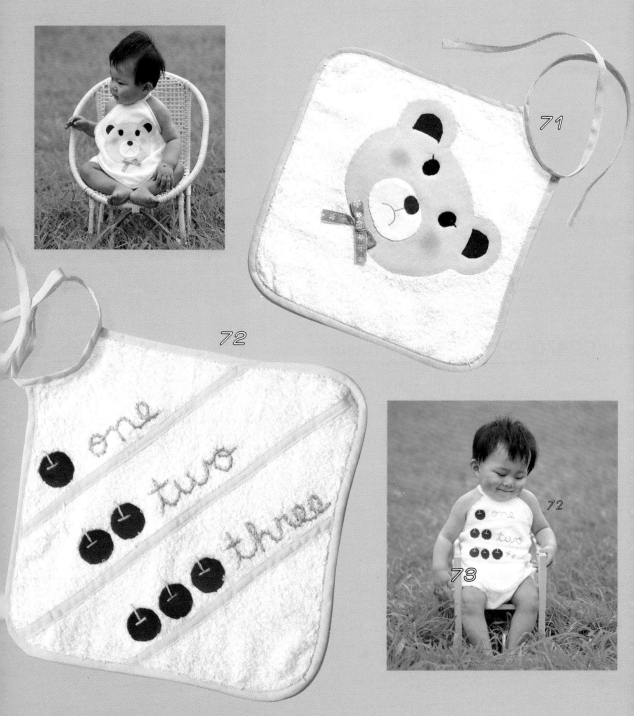

Directions: Teddy Bear (#71)—p. 58 and p. 105;
Counting Cherries (#72)—p. 59; Plain Colors (#74–76)—p. 58

TERRY TOYS

Babies #77 and #78, Dogs #79 and #80

74

75

76

80

77

79

78

Directions: Dogs—p. 100; Babies—p. 101

⟨74⟩⟨75⟩⟨76⟩ TERRY BIBS   shown on pp. 56–57

1. Cut cloth, if necessary to 10 ins. square, shape neck, as shown.

2. On #72 lay ½-in. binding flat across and stitch in place (p. 106), Fig. a.

3. On #71 appliqué Bear (p. 105), by hand or zigzag machine. On #72 do same with red circles for cherries (page 106). Finish both with touches of embroidery (pp. 105–106).

4. On all bibs cut twill tape in two and pin on side corners, Fig. b.

5. Bind all around, except neck, with 1-in. binding, stitching ends of tape in place at same time, Fig. c.

6. Bind neck, leaving at least 12 ins. for ties to be stitched together, Fig. d.

7. For #74–76 stitch remaining binding together and tie in bow. Sew bow on front with button, Fig. e.

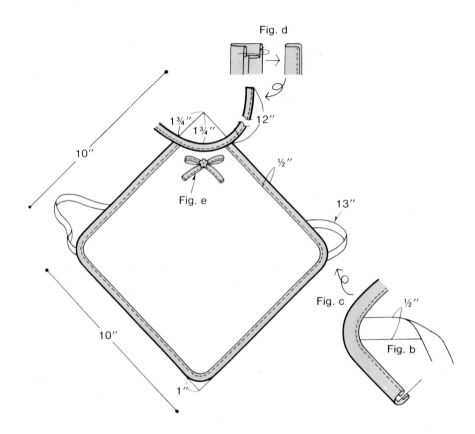

Fig. d

1¾″   1¾″   12″

10″   ½″

Fig. e

13″

10″

Fig. c   ½″

Fig. b

1″

Materials:	#74, 75, 76
Washcloth	1 in chosen color
Bias binding (1 in.)	Chosen color, 2¼ yds.
Twill tape (½ in.)	Chosen color, ¾ yd.
Flower button	1 white

Continued on page 105

Materials:	#71	#72
Washcloth	1 white	1 white
Cotton fabric	Scraps of tan, white, and brown	Scraps of red
Bias binding (1 in.)	Tan, 2 yds.	Yellow, 1 yd.
Bias binding (½ in.)		Yellow, 1 yd.
Cotton twill tape (½ in.)	White, ¾ yd.	White, ¾ yd.
Embroidered tape (½ in.)		Pink, ½ yd.
Six-strand embroidery floss, less than 1 skein each	Light green	Pink and brown

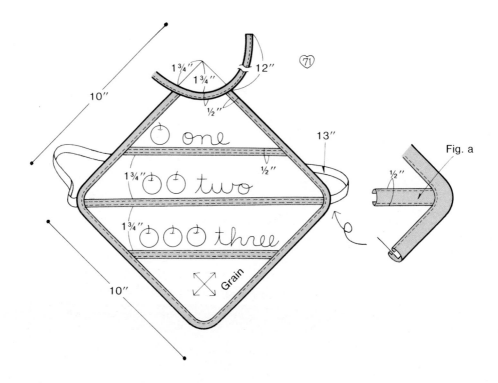

Continued on page 106

COVER-UP BIBS

BLUE WITH LACE #81,
PINK AND WHITE #82,
GREEN AND WHITE #83,
PINK WITH PRINT #84

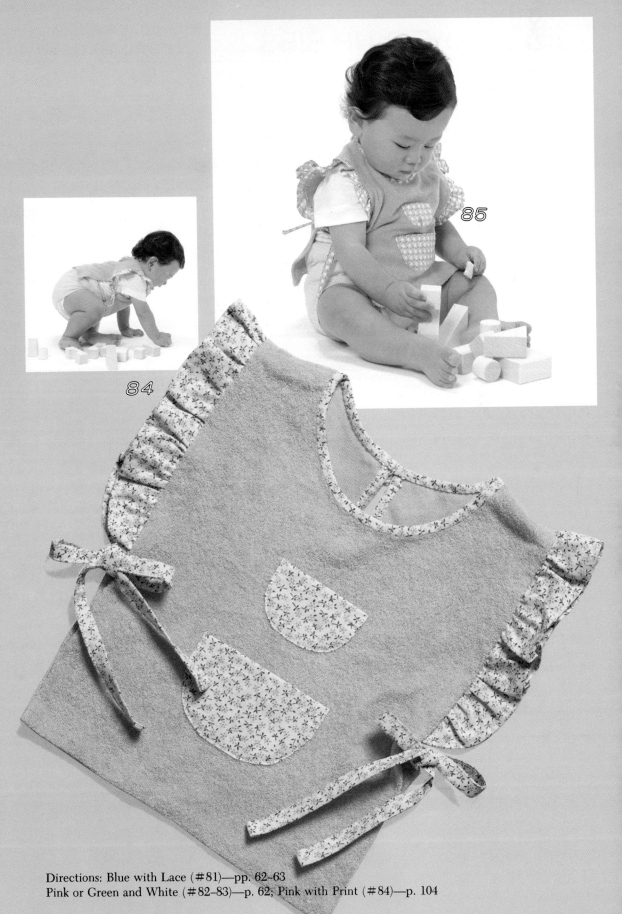

84

85

Directions: Blue with Lace (#81)—pp. 62–63
Pink or Green and White (#82–83)—p. 62; Pink with Print (#84)—p. 104

#81

1. Draw pattern full size from scaled diagram. Add ½ in. to all edges.
2. Cut fabric as in pattern layout.
3. Pleat lace to fit, stitch at hemline, Fig. a.
4. Hem edges, Fig. b, including ½-in. ribbon, 12 ins. in each side, Fig. c°
5. Bind neckline with terry bias, Fig. d.
6. Slip-stitch remaining ends of bias to make ties, Fig. e.
7. Tie bows and stitch in place, Fig. f.

#82–83

1. Draw pattern full size from scaled diagram. Add ½ in. to all edges except:
   Lay-on-fold lines
2. Hem side edges, Fig. a.°
3. Gather skirt to bib and seam together, including 12-in. white ribbon ties, Fig. b.
4. Make small pleat at top of bib, Fig. c.
5. Cut remaining white ribbon and sew at upper corners, Fig. d.
6. Hem top and bottom edges, Fig. e.°

° All terry edges may be hemmed with zigzag stitching or finished with zigzag and hemmed with straight stitch to avoid thickness of extra fold.

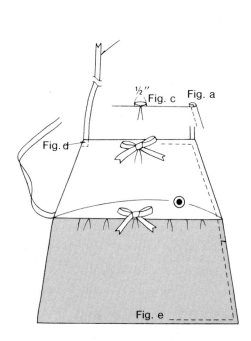

Fig. c Fig. a

Fig. d

Fig. e

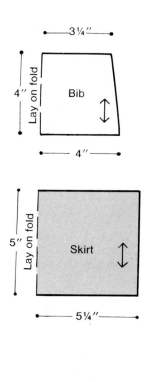

3¼″

Lay on fold

4″   Bib

4″

Lay on fold

5″   Skirt

5¼″

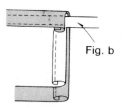

Fig. b

Materials:	#81	#82	#83
Terry cloth	Blue, 24 x 22 ins.	Pink, 6 x 12 ins.	Green, 6 x 12 ins.
Terry cloth, white		6 x 10 ins.	6 x 10 ins.
Satin ribbon (½ in.)	White, 1¼ yds. Blue, ½ yd.	White, 1¼ yds. Pink, ½ yd.	White, 1¼ yds. Yellow, ½ yd.
White lace (1½ ins.)	⅜ yd.		

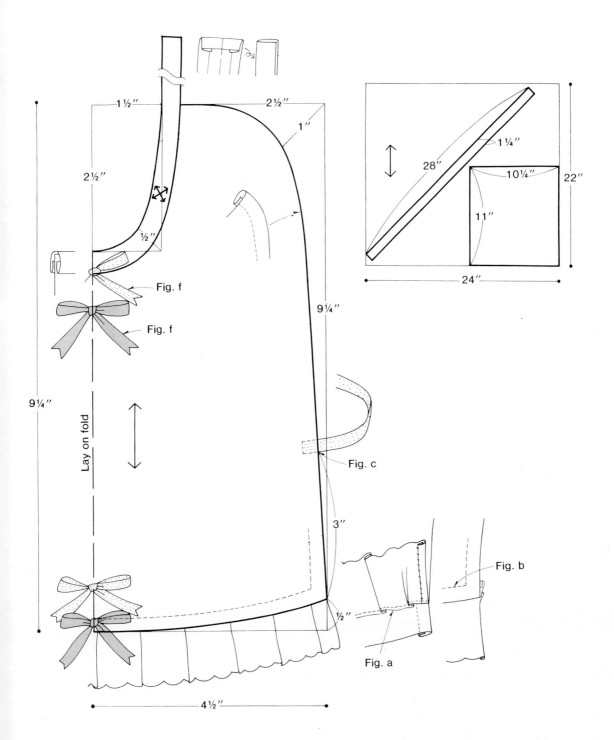

TERRY TOYS

HOUSE #86, AIRPLANE #87,
CAR #88, FLOWERPOT #89

86

88

87

89

Directions: House (#86)—p. 65;
Airplane (#87)—p. 66;
Car (#88)—p. 67; Flowerpot (#89)—p. 68

64

1. Trace patterns from pp. 65–68. Add ⅛-in. seam allowance to all edges except°:

    Appliqué pieces

    Lay-on-fold lines

2. Cut pieces in quantity marked on each and in colors shown in picture (p. 64).

3. Appliqué windows, doors, and decorative pieces, as shown for each toy, Fig. a.

4. Seam pieces together in order shown, Figs. b, c, etc.

5. Stuff such parts as chimney for house, wings and tail for airplane, etc. Stuff main body parts, working in order of Figs. d, e, etc.

6. Pin stuffed parts together and slip-stitch in place firmly. You may want to work back around these areas a second time for added strength.

° Terry cloth will stretch slightly and may break ordinary straight stitching in seams. It is advisable to use a wide zigzag machine stitch, covering entire ⅛-in. seam allowance. If working by hand, use an overcast stitch, taking whole ⅛-in. seam in each stitch, and fastening off firmly at the ends.

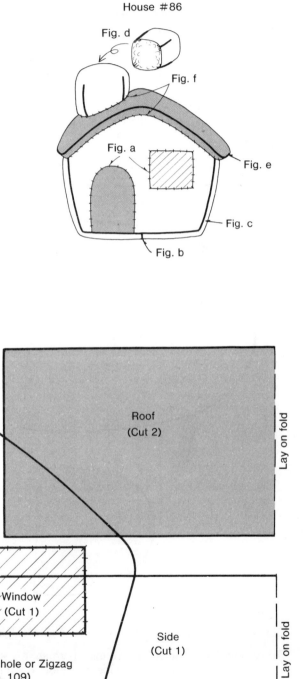

House #86

Fig. d

Fig. f

Fig. a

Fig. e

Fig. c

Fig. b

Chimney (Cut 1)

Roof (Cut 2)

Front & Back (Cut 2)

Window (Cut 1)

Door (Cut 1)

Buttonhole or Zigzag (See p. 109)

Side (Cut 1)

Lay on fold

Lay on fold

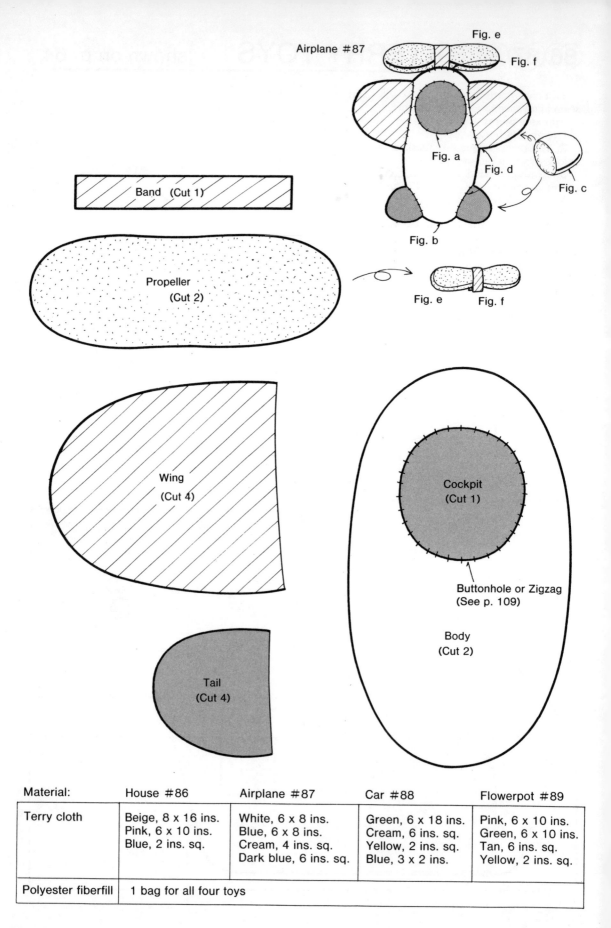

Airplane #87

Band (Cut 1)

Propeller
(Cut 2)

Fig. e
Fig. f

Fig. a

Fig. d

Fig. c

Fig. b

Fig. e   Fig. f

Wing
(Cut 4)

Cockpit
(Cut 1)

Buttonhole or Zigzag
(See p. 109)

Body
(Cut 2)

Tail
(Cut 4)

Material:	House #86	Airplane #87	Car #88	Flowerpot #89
Terry cloth	Beige, 8 x 16 ins. Pink, 6 x 10 ins. Blue, 2 ins. sq.	White, 6 x 8 ins. Blue, 6 x 8 ins. Cream, 4 ins. sq. Dark blue, 6 ins. sq.	Green, 6 x 18 ins. Cream, 6 ins. sq. Yellow, 2 ins. sq. Blue, 3 x 2 ins.	Pink, 6 x 10 ins. Green, 6 x 10 ins. Tan, 6 ins. sq. Yellow, 2 ins. sq.
Polyester fiberfill	1 bag for all four toys			

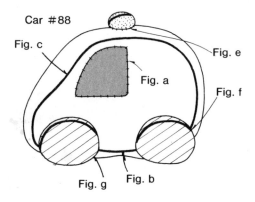

Car #88

Fig. c

Fig. e

Fig. a

Fig. f

Fig. g   Fig. b

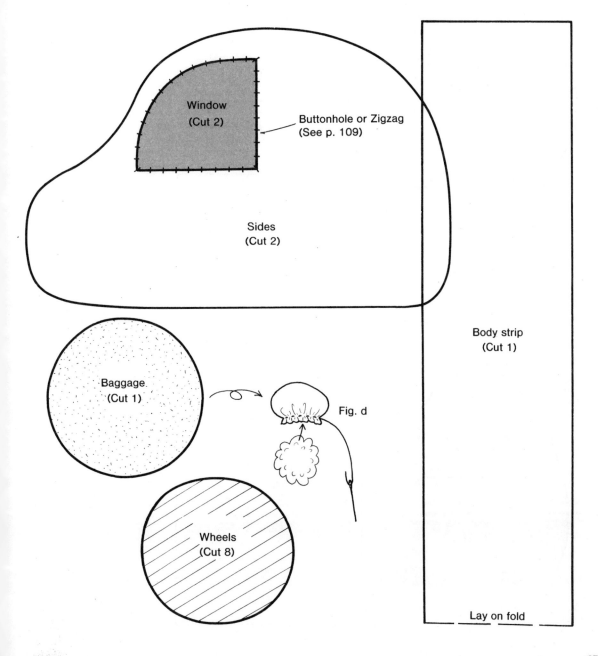

Window
(Cut 2)

Buttonhole or Zigzag
(See p. 109)

Sides
(Cut 2)

Body strip
(Cut 1)

Baggage
(Cut 1)

Fig. d

Wheels
(Cut 8)

Lay on fold

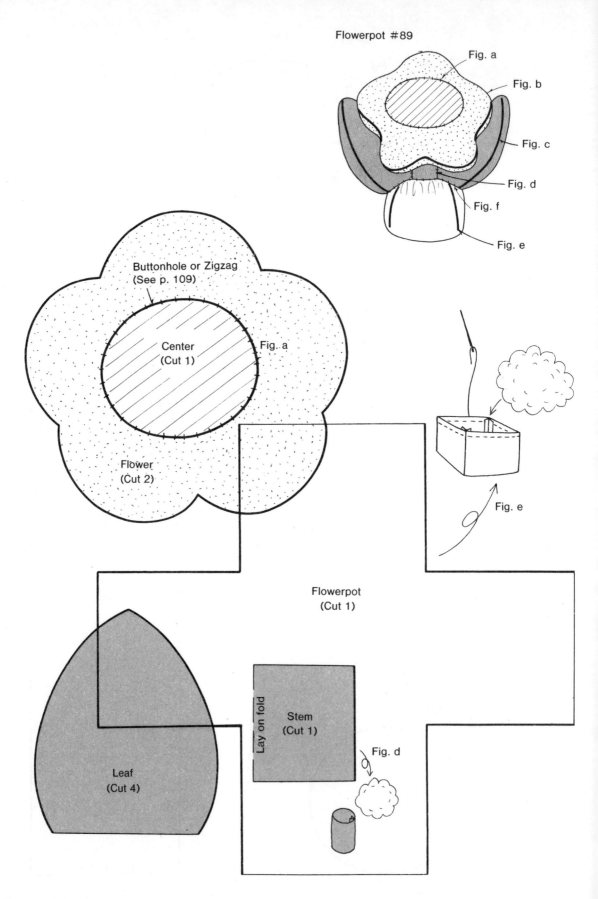

Flowerpot #89

Fig. a
Fig. b
Fig. c
Fig. d
Fig. f
Fig. e

Buttonhole or Zigzag
(See p. 109)

Center
(Cut 1)

Fig. a

Flower
(Cut 2)

Fig. e

Flowerpot
(Cut 1)

Lay on fold

Stem
(Cut 1)

Fig. d

Leaf
(Cut 4)

68

1. Trace patterns, adding ½ in. seam to straight back edge of A only.

2. Lay sole B on fold of all three fabrics and cut, for both shoes.

3. Cut side A twice in each fabric for both shoes.

4. Iron interfacing on wrong side of all fabric pieces. Lay lining pieces with wrong side against interfacing and pin.

5. Seam backs, stitch flat, Fig. a.

6. Cut eyelet in two and gather to fit top edge of each shoe. Bind in place, Fig. b.

7. Cut ribbon in four pieces and attach, Fig. c.

8. Bind edge of A and B separately. Overcast firmly together by hand, Fig. d.

Materials:
(Fabrics 36 to 45 ins. wide)

White cotton satin	⅛ yd.
White cotton lining	⅛ yd.
Iron-on interfacing	⅛ yd.
White eyelet edging (¾ in.)	1¼ yds.
White ribbon (½ in.)	1 yd.
White bias binding (½ in.)	2¼ yds.

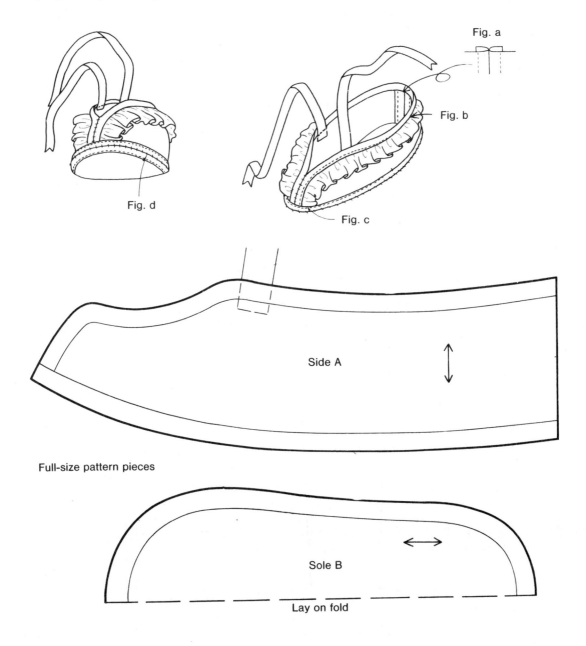

Fig. a

Fig. b

Fig. c

Fig. d

Side A

Full-size pattern pieces

Sole B

Lay on fold

1. Draw patterns full size from scaled diagrams (see p.107). Add ½-in. seam allowance to all edges of all pieces except:

Lay-on-fold lines of C, F, and H.

2. Follow arrows and fold lines to lay patterns on fabric and cut.

3. Mark all folded centers and *fold* and *center* lines of A, E, and G, with a clip at ends.

4. Seam shoulders A to C and B to D, Fig. a.

5. Seam A-C to B-D.

6. Gather E to fit A-B and seam together, Fig. b.

7. Gather F to fit C-D and seam together, Fig. b.

8. Gather 1½ yds. of eyelet X to fit around A and C, from front to front. Cover with Z, miter corners and stitch in place, Fig. c.

9. Cover inside seams with bias binding, Fig. d.

10. Gather 18 ins. of Y to fit around neck, center front to center front. Seam and cover with binding, Fig. e.

11. Cover yoke with embroidered flowers. Run ribbon in beading, Fig. f.

12. Seam E to F at sides, edge-stitch seams, Fig. g.

13. Gather sleeves and seam into armholes, Fig. h.

14. Cut two 16-in. pieces of eyelet Y and gather to sleeve ends, seam and cover with binding. Cut two 6-in. pieces of elastic and stretch to fit sleeves, stitch 1 in. from lower edge, Fig. j.

15. Seam G to H at sides and gather 2 yds. of X to bottom edge, seam and finish with binding, Fig. k. Finish lower edge of E-F with 2½ yds. of X.

16. Turn back front edges on *fold line* and hem. Sew on snaps and cover with decorative buttons, Fig. l.

17. Gather G-H to match E-F and bind upper edge, join by hand. If dress is used for Christening, the lower ruffle may be removed later, Fig. m.

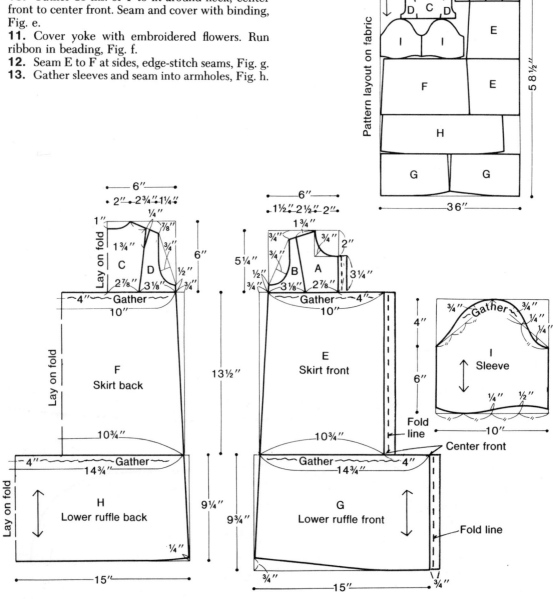

Materials:
(Fabrics 36 to 45 ins. wide)

	Dress	Bonnet
White cotton satin	1⅝ yds.	⅜ yd.
White cotton lining		⅜ yd.
Iron-on interfacing		⅜ yd.
White eyelet edging (X) (2 ins.)	6 yds.	
White eyelet edging (Y) (1 in.)	1½ yds.	¾ yd.
White eyelet beading* (Z) (½ in.)	1 yd.	½ yd.
Pink satin ribbon (¼ in.)	2 yds.	¾ yd.
White bias binding (½ in.)	6 yds.	¾ yd.
Soft elastic (¼ in.)	⅜ yd.	
Small pearl buttons	8	
Snap fasteners (small)	8	

Six-strand embroidery floss in yellow-green, dark and light blue, dark and light pink, and dark and light yellow, less than 1 skein each.

* Beading: Eyelet or lace with slots for threading ribbon.

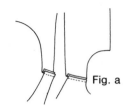

Fig. a

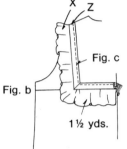

Fig. b   Fig. c

1½ yds.

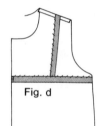

Fig. d

Y 18″

Fig. e

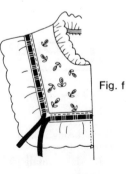

Fig. f

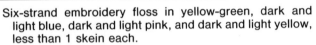

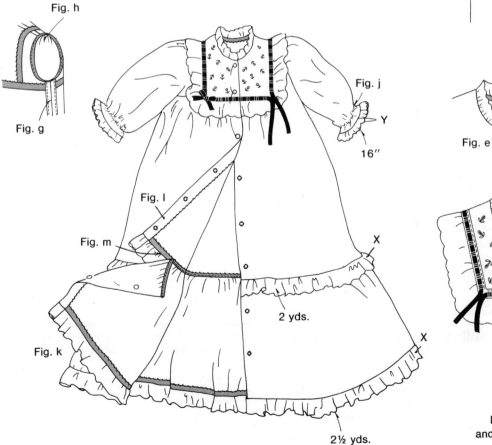

Fig. h

Fig. g

Fig. j

Y

16″

Fig. l

Fig. m

X

2 yds.

Fig. k

X

2½ yds.

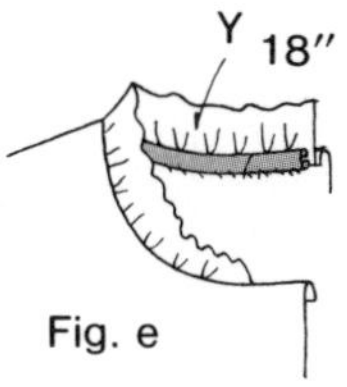

Lazy Daisy
and Stem Stitch

⑥ BONNET

shown on p. 5

1. Draw patterns full size from scaled diagrams (see p.107). Add ½-in. seam allowance to all edges of all pieces except:
  Lay-on-fold lines of A, B, and C.
  Lower bound edges of A and C.
2. Lay all three pieces on fold of fabric and lining and cut. Lay B on fold of interfacing and cut. Clip fold ends to mark.
3. Cover brim and bonnet sides with embroidered flowers.

4. Iron interfacing on wrong side of brim. Gather Y to edge. Seam lining to brim with eyelet between, Fig. a.
5. Seam A to B, cover with Z, Fig. b. Cut ribbon in two pieces, thread in Z and tie on top.
6. Gather A at neck and upper edge, seam to C. Repeat with lining A and C. Hand-finish lining over brim seam. Bind neck edge, Fig. c.

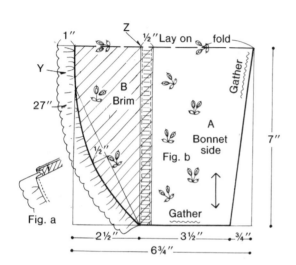

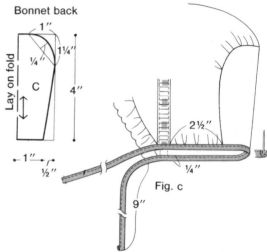

Lazy Daisy
and Stem Stitch

④ PINK BAG

shown on p. 4

1. Draw pattern full size from scaled diagram (see p.107). Do not add seam allowance.
2. Cut elastic in half. Sew each piece on dotted line, through both organdy and lining, stretching elastic, Fig. a.
3. Make small ribbon loop on both front and back, Fig. b.
4. Bind sides of all four layers together, Fig. c.
5. Make three petals from pattern on p. 7. Gather them and bind with short piece of bias binding, Fig. d.
6. Bind top edge. Run 48 ins. of ribbon in loops and knot at ends, Fig. e.

Materials: for bag only
(Fabrics 36 to 45 ins. wide)

Pink organdy—left over from dress	
Pink cotton lining—left over from dress	
Pink bias binding (½ in.)	1 yd.
Pink satin ribbon (¼ in.)	1½ yds.
Soft elastic (¼ in.)	¼ yd.

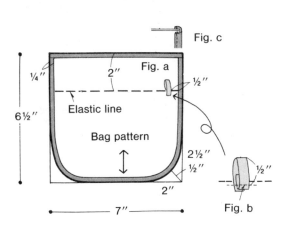

Fig. c

Fig. a

¼″

2″

½″

6½″

Elastic line

Bag pattern

2½″
½″

½″

Fig. b

2″

7″

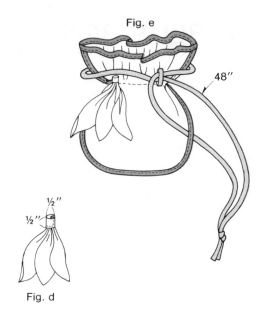

Fig. e

48″

½″

½″

½″

Fig. d

♡7♡8 **WHITE BONNETS**   shown on p. 8

1. Draw patterns full size from scaled diagrams (see p.107). Add ½-in. seam allowance to all edges of all pieces except:
   Lay-on-fold line of B.
   Lower edges of both pieces.
2. Pin and cut fabric and lining by pattern pieces.
3. Mark folded center on B and center line on A with a clip at ends.
4. Seam B to A pieces in both outer fabric and lining, easing B as necessary around curves, Fig. a.
5. Gather two 18-in. pieces of eyelet to fit front edge (on #8 lay the narrow piece on top). Curve the gathers to form a point at each end, Fig. b.
6. Seam lining to bonnet with gathered eyelet between, Fig. c.
7. Gather lower edges and bind, Fig. d.
8. Sew on ribbon with bows at sides, Fig. e.

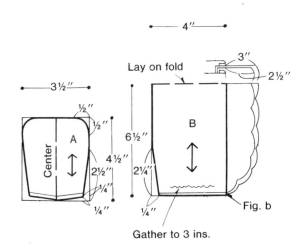

4″

3½″

Lay on fold

3″

2½″

½″

½″

A

Center

6½″

B

4½″

2½″
¼″

2¼″

¼″

¼″

Fig. b

Gather to 3 ins.

Materials:
(Fabric leftovers)

	#7	#8
White cotton broadcloth	5 x 20 ins.	
White cotton satin		5 x 20 ins.
White cotton lining	5 x 20 ins.	5 x 20 ins.
White eyelet edging (3½ ins.)	1 yd.	½ yd.
White eyelet edging (3 ins.)		½ yd.
White bias binding (½ in.)	¼ yd.	¼ yd.
White satin ribbon (½ in.)	1 yd.	1 yd.

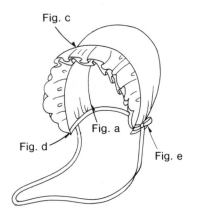

Fig. c

Fig. a

Fig. d

Fig. e

73

1. Draw patterns full size from scaled diagrams (see p.107). Add ½-in. seam allowance to all edges of all pieces. Mark centers with clips.

2. Cut A, B, and C from piqué. Cut C and D from lining.

3. Make nineteen 1/16-in. pin tucks in A (taking up a total of ⅛ in. per tuck), Fig. a.

4. Cut eyelet into two pieces. Gather each to 12½ ins.

5. Seam one piece of eyelet to each side of A. Seam A to B, Fig. b.

6. Seam A-B to C and lining D to C, easing around curves as necessary, Fig. c.

7. Lay pleats as marked at neck edge of both bonnet and lining. Seam bonnet to lining all around, leaving small opening on neck edge for turning. Turn right side out and topstitch, Fig. d.

8. Sew on ribbon with bows at sides, Fig. e.

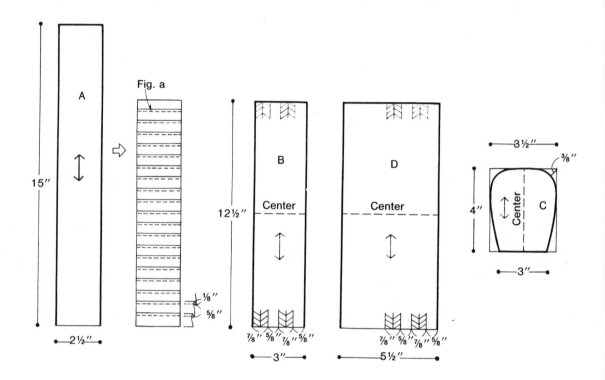

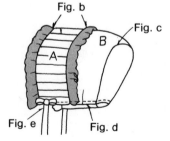

Materials:
(Fabric leftovers)

Blue lightweight piqué	7 x 24 ins.
Blue cotton lining	7 x 20 ins.
White eyelet edging (1 in.)	1 yd.
Blue satin ribbon (½ in.)	1 yd.

⑫ LARGE TIE-ON BIB shown on p. 12

1. Trace pattern pieces A-B and B. Add ¼-in. seam allowance only to straight edge of B.
2. Lay A-B on straight-grain fold of flannel and B on straight-grain fold of voile to cut.
3. Mark centers by clipping ends of folds.
4. Stitch eyelet (not gathered except slightly around upper curve) to inner line and along edge of voile, Fig. a.
5. Embroider flowers on voile, as shown.
6. Lay voile wrong side down on flannel and bind lower edges together, Fig. b.
7. Bind from neck around upper curved edge of flannel only, leaving 12-in. ties, Fig. c.

8. Topstitch voile to flannel around outer edge, Fig. d.
9. Bind neck edge, both layers, leaving 10-in. ties, Fig. e.
10. Tie ribbon bows and stitch in place, Fig. f.

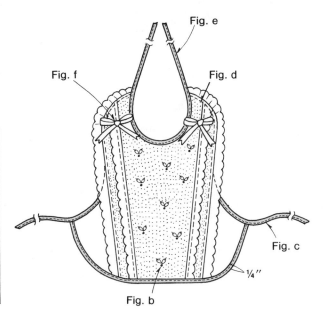

Fig. e
Fig. f
Fig. d
Fig. c
¼"
Fig. b

Materials:

White outing flannel	12-ins. sq.
White cotton voile	12 x 8 ins.
White bias binding (½-in.)	2½ yds.
White satin ribbon (¼ in.)	½ yd.
White eyelet edging (¾ in.)	1½ yds.
Six-strand embroidery floss in yellow and green, less than 1 skein each	

⑬ HEART-SHAPED BIB shown on p. 12

1. Trace pattern pieces A-B and C. Do not add seam allowance.
2. Lay A-B on straight-grain fold of flannel and C on straight-grain fold of voile to cut.
3. Mark centers by clipping ends of folds.
4. Gather eyelet and stitch to lower edges of voile, Fig. g.
5. Stitch narrow ribbon along edge and cover

with Herringbone and French Knot stitches (or use picot ribbon), Fig. h.
6. Embroider voile with French Knots, as shown.
7. Bind lower and upper curved edges of flannel, leaving 12-in. ties, Fig. k.
8. Lay voile wrong side down on flannel and bind neck edge, leaving 10-in. ties, Fig. l.
9. Tie ribbon bow and stitch in place, Fig. m.

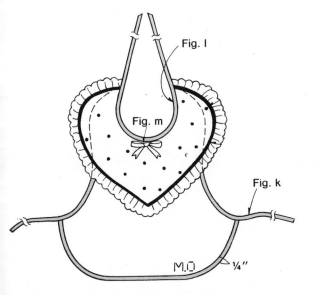

Fig. l
Fig. m
Fig. k
M.O
¼"

Materials:

White outing flannel	12-ins. sq.
White cotton voile	10 x 8 ins.
White bias binding (½ in.)	2½ yds.
White satin ribbon (½-in.)	¼ yd.
White satin ribbon (¼ in.) (or narrow picot ribbon)	⅝ yd.
White eyelet edging (¾ in.)	1 yd.
Six-strand embroidery floss, red, less than 1 skein.	

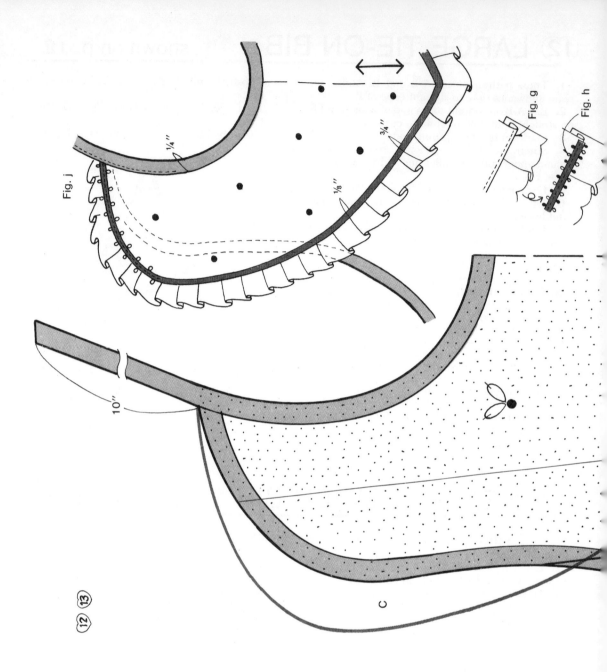

Fig. j

Fig. g

Fig. h

1/4''

3/4''

1/8''

10''

12 13

C

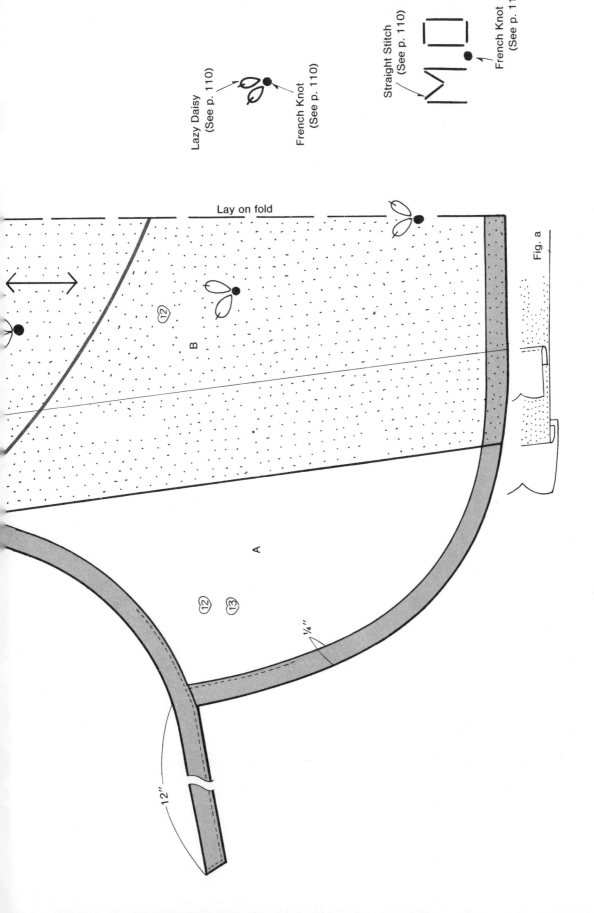

Lazy Daisy
(See p. 110)

French Knot
(See p. 110)

Straight Stitch
(See p. 110)

French Knot
(See p. 110)

Lay on fold

Fig. a

B

A

12

12   13

¼"

12"

1. Draw pattern full size from scaled diagram (see p. 107). Add ½-in. seam allowance to all edges except:
　　Neck edge.
2. Cut one from fabric and one from lining.
3. Embroider flowers on outer fabric, as shown.

4. Gather eyelet to fit outer edge and incorporate in seam between bib and lining, Fig. a.
5. Cut two 12-in. pieces of bias, fold and stitch. Hand-sew at placement marks, Fig. b.
6. Bind neck edge, leaving tie ends, Fig. c.

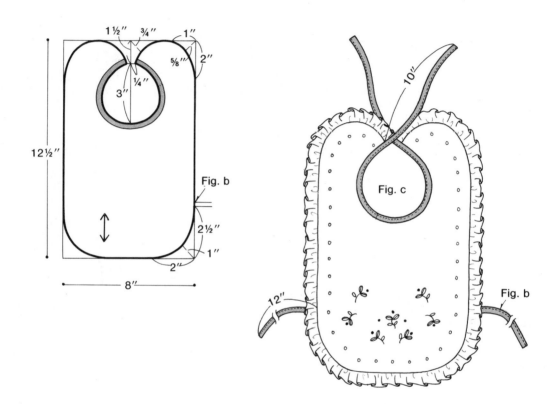

Fig. b

Fig. c

Fig. b

Fig. a

Materials:
(Fabrics 36 to 45 ins. wide)

White cotton fabric	¼ yd.
White lining fabric	¼ yd.
White eyelet edging (¾ in.)	1⅝ yds.
Pink bias binding (½ in.)	1½ yds.
Six-strand embroidery floss in yellow, pink, and green, less than 1 skein each.	

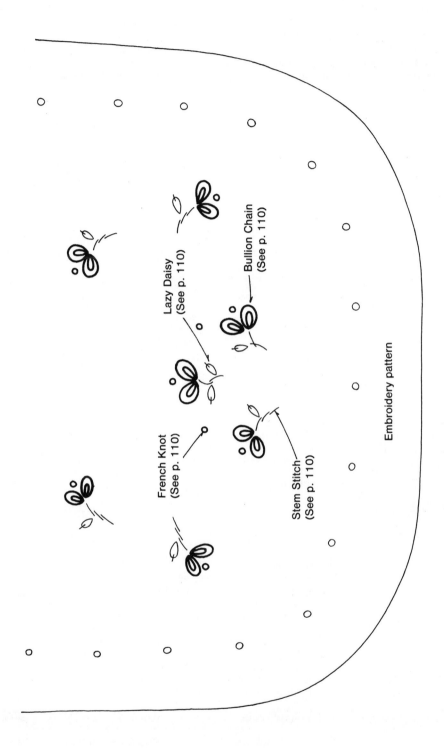

Lazy Daisy
(See p. 110)

Bullion Chain
(See p. 110)

French Knot
(See p. 110)

Stem Stitch
(See p. 110)

Embroidery pattern

1. Trace patterns from page 81. Do not add seam allowance.

2. Cut booties and lining from felt—eight uppers and four soles for each pair.

3. Stitch Tyrolean trim or grosgrain ribbon in place on one layer as shown, Fig. a.

4. Sew front seam with hand overcast, Fig. b.

5. Decorate #23 with embroidery and #24 with beads, Fig. c.

6. Sew back seams same as front. Place small ribbon loop at back to be sewn between bootie and lining, Fig. d.

7. Glue linings into both uppers and soles, finishing upper edge with buttonhole stitch, Fig. e.

8. Sew soles to uppers with buttonhole stitch, Fig. f.

9. Sew Velcro® dots at closing and sew buttons on top, Fig. g.

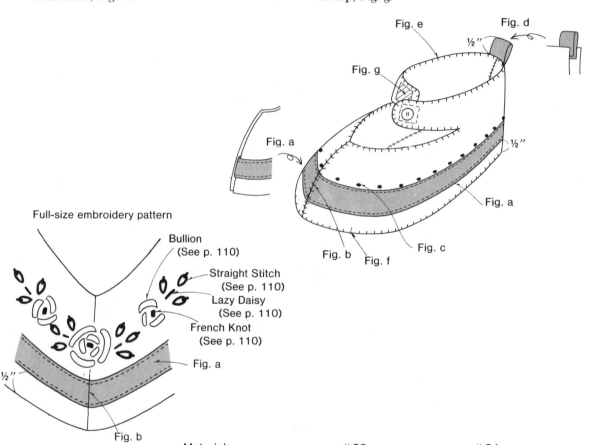

Fig. e

Fig. d

Fig. g

Fig. a

½ ″

½ ″

Fig. a

Fig. b   Fig. f   Fig. c

Full-size embroidery pattern

Bullion
(See p. 110)

Straight Stitch
(See p. 110)

Lazy Daisy
(See p. 110)

French Knot
(See p. 110)

Fig. a

½ ″

Fig. b

Materials:	#23	#24
Felt	White, 12 x 16 ins.	Blue, 12 x 16 ins.
Tyrolean trim (⅝ in.)		¾ yd.
Grosgrain (½ in.)	White, ¾ yd.	
Transparent beads		48
Buttons (⅜ in.)	2	2
Velcro® dots	White, 2	Blue, 2
Six-strand embroidery floss, less than 1 skein each	Green and white	Blue
Fabric glue or thin iron-on bonding agent.		

80

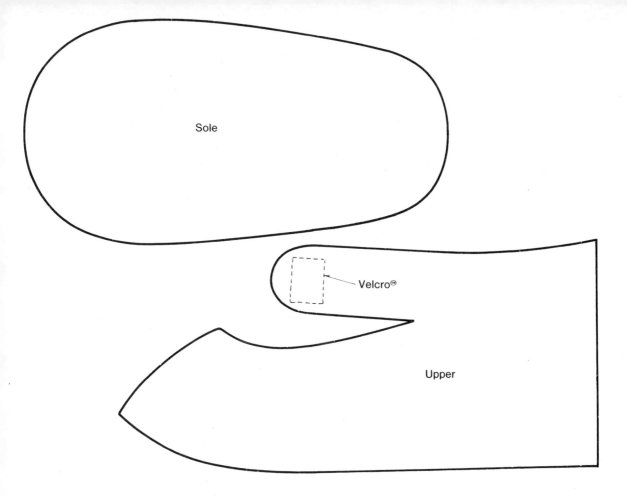

Sole

Velcro®

Upper

⟨18⟩⟨19⟩⟨20⟩ MITTENS   shown on p. 16

1. Trace patterns from page 82. Add ¼-in. seams to all edges except:
 Add ⅜-in. hem to straight edge of #18.

2. Cut four pieces from main fabric for each pair of mittens.

3. Decorate one side of each mitten with appli-

Materials:	#18	#19	#20
Jersey, white	2 x 4 ins.		12 ins.
Jersey, pink	12 ins. sq.		
Jersey, print		12 ins. sq.	
Pink lace flowers*		½ yd.	10
Pink lace (⅜ in.)		¾ yd.	
Pink ribbon (¼ in.)	½ yd.		¼ yd.
Pink ribbon (⅛ in.)		¼ yd.	
Elastic (⅛ in.)	10 ins.	10 ins.	10 ins.
Six-strand embroidery floss, less than 1 skein each	Pink, blue, yellow, ash brown, and moss green		Pink and moss green

* There is a type of floral embroidery sold by the yard (or packaged) that can be cut apart for floral motifs or used in one piece like lace edging.

qué, lace, or embroidery, as shown. *Note:* on #18 there are two motifs, both shown full size.

4. Cut elastic into four 2½-in. pieces for each pair of mittens.

5. On #18 hem lower edge, Fig. a. Stretch elastic and sew ⅜ in. from upper edge of hem, Fig. b.

6. Sew elastic with single-turned hem and lace on other mittens, Fig. c.

7. For each mitten, seam one decorated to one plain piece around the curved edge, backstitching at each end.

8. Tie ribbon bows and hand-stitch in place.

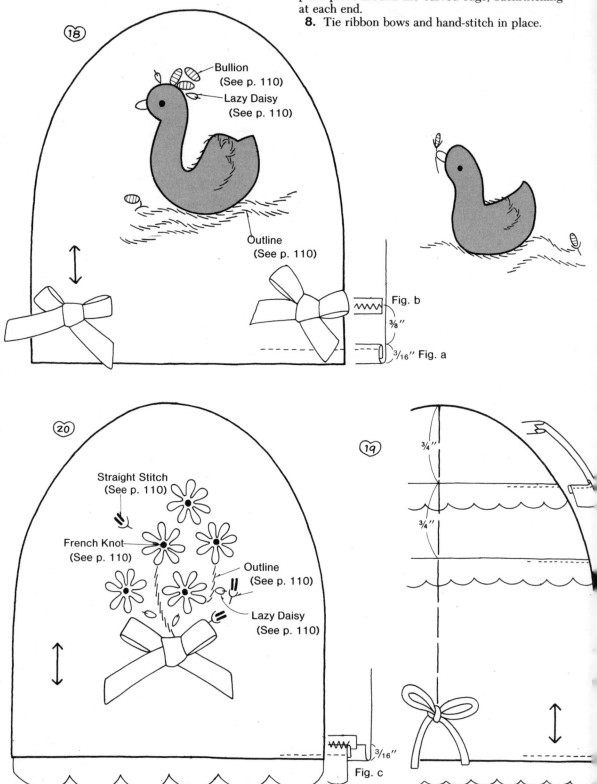

18

Bullion
(See p. 110)

Lazy Daisy
(See p. 110)

Outline
(See p. 110)

Fig. b

⅜"

³/₁₆" Fig. a

20

Straight Stitch
(See p. 110)

French Knot
(See p. 110)

Outline
(See p. 110)

Lazy Daisy
(See p. 110)

Fig. c

³/₁₆"

19

¾"

¾"

1. Draw patterns full size from scaled diagrams (see p. 00). Add ¼-in. seam allowance to side and shoulder only.

2. Gather two 13-in. pieces of 1¼-in. eyelet, seam them along diagonal lines on left front, and topstitch, Fig. a.

3. Seam sides and shoulders, Fig. b.

4. Gather a 40-in. piece of 1¼-in. eyelet and sew it to neck with binding, Fig. c.

5. Finish lower edge with a 42-in. piece of 1¼-in. eyelet, gathered and attached inside with binding, Fig. d.

6. Cut 1¾-in. eyelet in two, gather to fit armholes, and attach inside with binding, tapering ends at underarm, Figs. d and e.

7. Fold and stitch remaining bias, cut in two, and attach as ties, Fig. f.

8. Cut ribbon into 9-in. pieces and attach as shown.

Materials:
(Fabrics 36 to 45 ins. wide)

Quilted print fabric	⅜ yd.
White eyelet edging (1¾ ins.)	1 yd.
White eyelet edging (1¼ ins.)	3 yds.
Yellow bias binding (½ in.)	3 yds.
Yellow satin ribbon (⅝ in.)	1 yd.

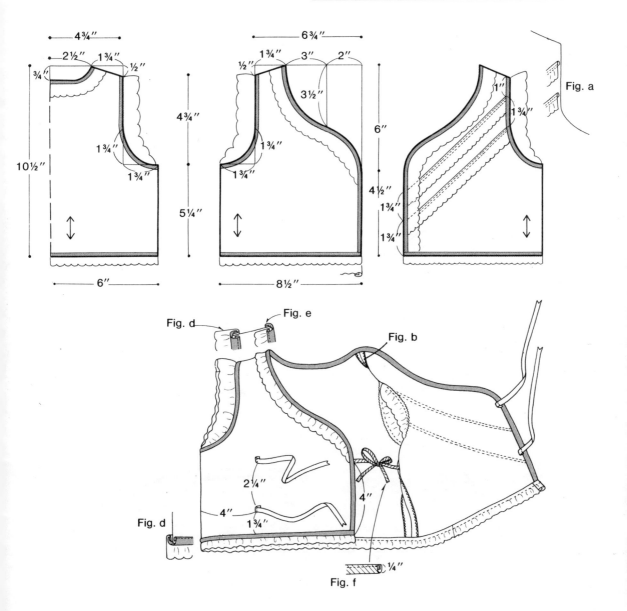

Fig. a

Fig. b

Fig. d

Fig. e

Fig. d

Fig. f

1. Trace patterns from page 84. Add ¼-in. seam allowance to back edge of upper only.

2. Cut four uppers and two soles in both main fabric and lining for each pair of booties.

3. Cut two soles in batting for each pair.

4. Embroider fronts, Fig. a, using full-size diagram.

5. Cut ribbon in half and pin in place for ties, Fig. b.

6. Seam back of uppers in both main fabric and lining. Place wrong sides together.

7. Bind around top of bootie, Fig. c.

8. Place batting between sole fabric and lining, baste or stitch, then bind to uppers, Fig. d.

Materials:	#29	#30
Top	White cotton, 12 x 14 ins.	Blue cotton, 12 x 14 ins.
Lining	White, 12 x 14 ins.	Blue, 12 x 14 ins.
Batting	6 x 6 ins.	6 x 6 ins.
Bias binding (½ in.)	White, 1¼ yds.	Blue, 1¼ yds.
Satin ribbon (½ in.)	White, ¾ yd.	Blue, ¾ yd.
Six-strand embroidery floss, less than 1 skein each	Pink and blue	Blue and green

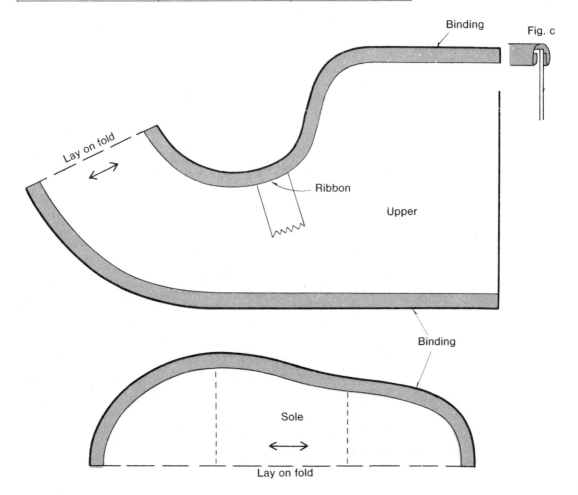

Binding

Fig. c

Lay on fold

Ribbon

Upper

Binding

Sole

Lay on fold

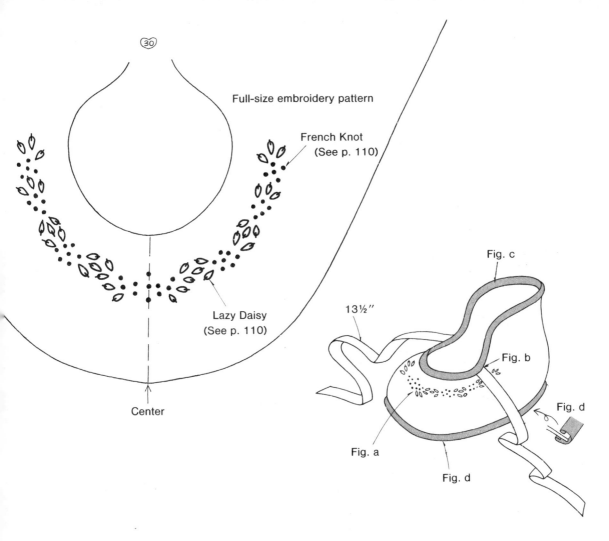

30

Full-size embroidery pattern

French Knot
(See p. 110)

Lazy Daisy
(See p. 110)

Center

Fig. c

13½″

Fig. b

Fig. d

Fig. a

Fig. d

31 32 FLANNEL BOOTIES
PRINT #31 AND PINK EMBROIDERED #32   shown on p. 21

1. Trace patterns from page 86. Add ¼-in. seam allowance on all edges except folds.

2. Cut two each of all three pieces for each pair of booties. Cut same in lining. Cut batting insoles without seam allowance.

3. Embroider tongue of #32, using full-size diagram, Fig. a.

4. Seam linings to fabric of uppers and tongues on all but lower edge. Turn right side out, Fig. b.

5. Seam lined uppers and tongues to unlined soles, matching points A and B, Fig. c.

6. Lay batting insole inside each bootie. Turn under seam allowance of sole lining and slip-stitch to cover raw seams.

7. Cut ribbon in half and stitch in place, Fig. d.

Materials:	#31	#32
Top	Print, 12 x 10 ins.	Pink, 12 x 10 ins.
Lining	White, 12 x 10 ins.	Print, 12 x 10 ins.
Batting	6 x 6 ins.	6 x 6 ins.
Satin ribbon (½ in.)	Pink, ¾ yd.	Pink, ¾ yd.
Six-strand embroidery floss, less than 1 skein each		Pink, rose, and light green

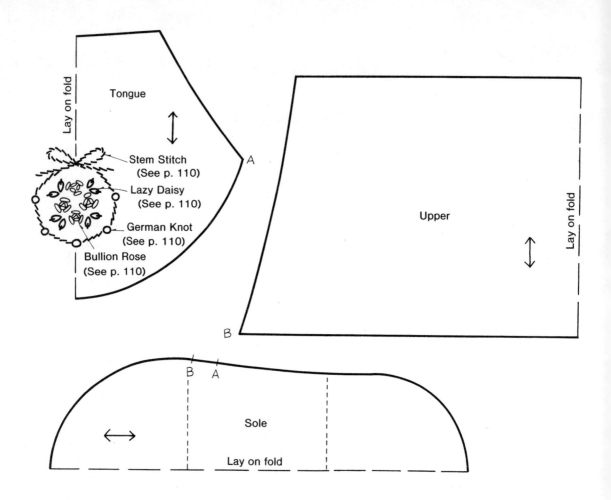

Tongue

Lay on fold

Stem Stitch
(See p. 110)

Lazy Daisy
(See p. 110)

German Knot
(See p. 110)

Bullion Rose
(See p. 110)

A

B

Upper

Lay on fold

B A

Sole

Lay on fold

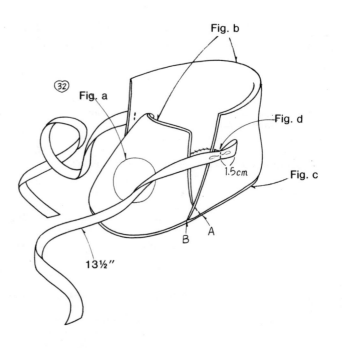

Fig. b

㉜ Fig. a

Fig. d

1.5cm

Fig. c

B A

13½″

Continued from page 51

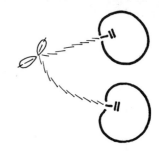

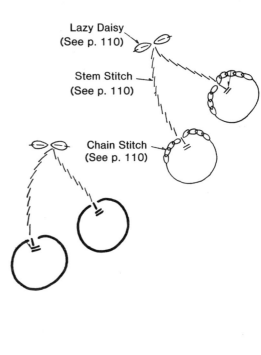

Lazy Daisy
(See p. 110)

Stem Stitch
(See p. 110)

Chain Stitch
(See p. 110)

㊿

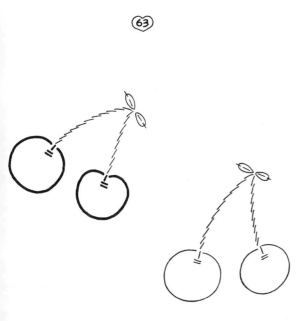

GINGHAM BOOTIES

33 34 SMALL CHECK #33 AND MEDIUM CHECK #34   shown on p. 21

1. Trace patterns from page 86. Add seam allowance to back of upper and all around band and loop, except on fold line.
2. Cut two each of all pieces for each pair of booties, except four of strap. Cut two each of lining for uppers and soles.
3. Cut two band interfacings on straight grain. Cut two insoles of batting. Cut approximately 20 ins. of 1-in. wide bias for binding, as in pattern layout.

4. Seam bands and interfacing, leaving small opening in one side to turn. Turn, work buttonhole, Fig. a.
5. Seam loops and turn, Fig. b.
6. Seam back. Bind uppers and linings together, Fig. c.
7. Stitch loop at back.
8. Layer insole between sole and lining.
9. Bind soles to uppers, Fig. d.
10. Sew button in place.

Materials:	#33	#34
Top	Small gingham check, 20 x 15 ins.	Medium gingham check, 20 x 15 ins.
Lining	Red cotton, 16 x 8 ins.	Navy cotton, 16 x 8 ins.
Band interfacing	White cotton, 2 x 8 ins.	White cotton, 2 x 8 ins.
Batting	6 x 6 ins.	6 x 6 ins.
Buttons (½ in.)	2	2

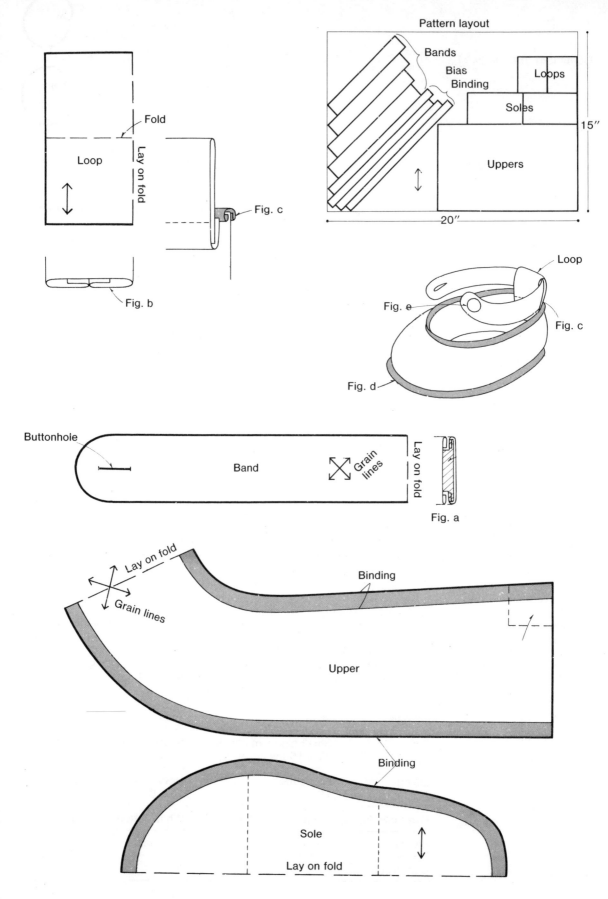

Pattern layout

Bands

Bias Binding

Loops

Soles

Uppers

15″

20″

Fold

Loop

Lay on fold

Fig. c

Fig. b

Loop

Fig. e

Fig. c

Fig. d

Buttonhole

Band

Grain lines

Lay on fold

Fig. a

Lay on fold

Grain lines

Binding

Upper

Binding

Sole

Lay on fold

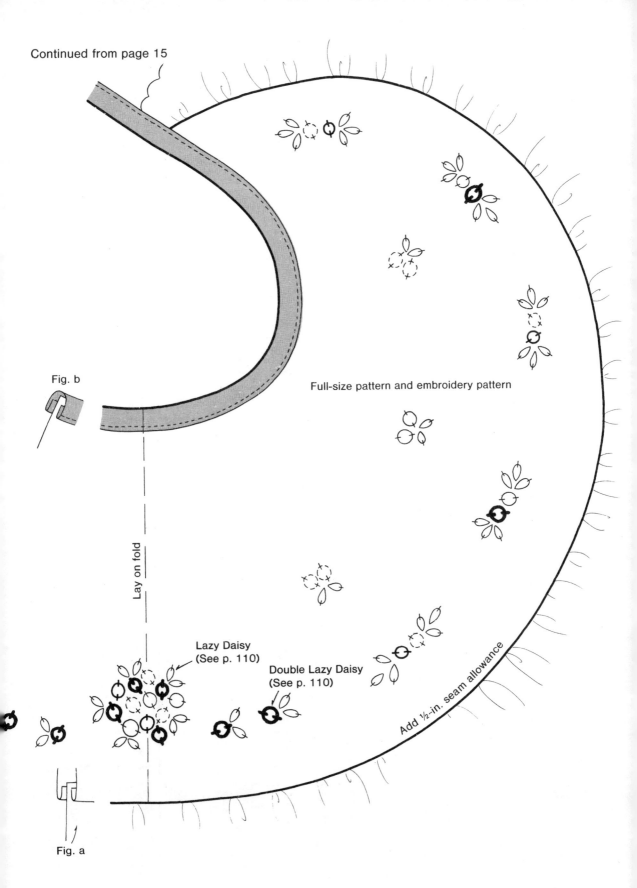

Continued from page 15

Fig. b

Full-size pattern and embroidery pattern

Lay on fold

Lazy Daisy
(See p. 110)

Double Lazy Daisy
(See p. 110)

Add ½-in. seam allowance

Fig. a

1. Trace full-size patterns from pages 92–93 for appliqué, no seam allowance necessary if worked on zigzag machine. For hand appliqué allow ¼ in. all around each piece. Bird's wing and rabbit's and bear's floppy ears will need ¼-in. seam allowance.

2. Cut blue piece 39½ by 29½ ins.

3. Cut appliqué pieces according to colors on page 29 and work onto blue piece. Cut two each for wing and floppy ears, seam around, and turn right side out. Sew in place. Finish with embroidery.

4. Cut strips of white, 7¼ by 52 ins. and 7¼ by 43 ins., miter corners, as shown, for frame of top. Topstitch around picture panel.

5. Cut back, 43 by 52 ins. in white for comforter, or with seam, as shown, for blanket cover.

6. Seam front to back, leaving one long side open about 46 ins. for comforter. For blanket cover leave opening in center seam to be overcast by hand after blanket is inserted. Insert batting through side of comforter.

7. Sew buttons through for blanket cover, to hold in place between washings.

8. For comforter sew buttons in place and use thread to make ties along various seams to secure batting.

Materials:
Fabrics 45 ins. wide broadcloth

White	3 yds.
Blue	1 ¼ yds.
Two shades green	⅜ yd. each
Pink	½ yd.
Dark pink, yellow, two shades tan, pink stripe, and print	Small amount each
Pink ribbon (⅜ in.)	1 ¼ yds.
Six-strand embroidery floss, less than 1 skein each of tan, pink, brown, lavender, pink, blue, and green.	
Pellon® Fleece	4 x 6 ins.
Thick batting (or) Baby blanket	45 x 54 ins.

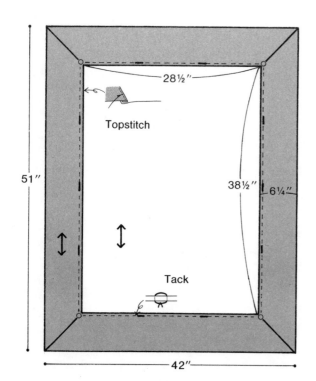

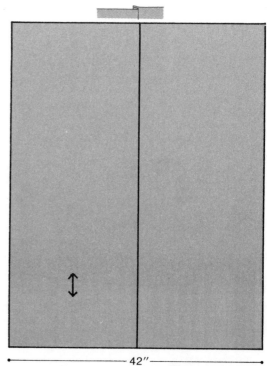

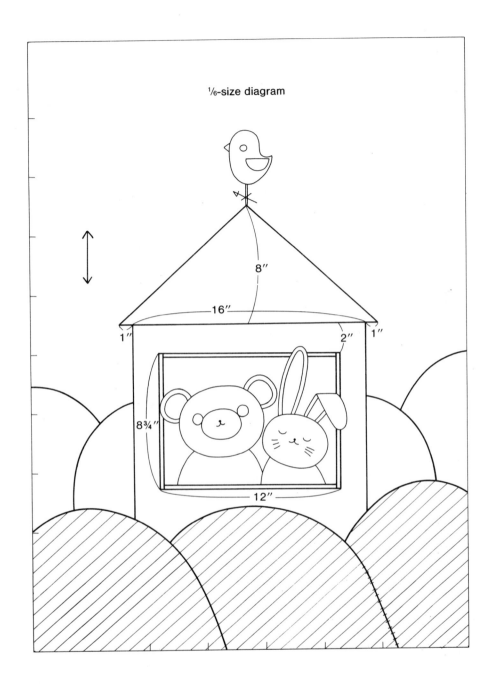

¹⁄₆-size diagram

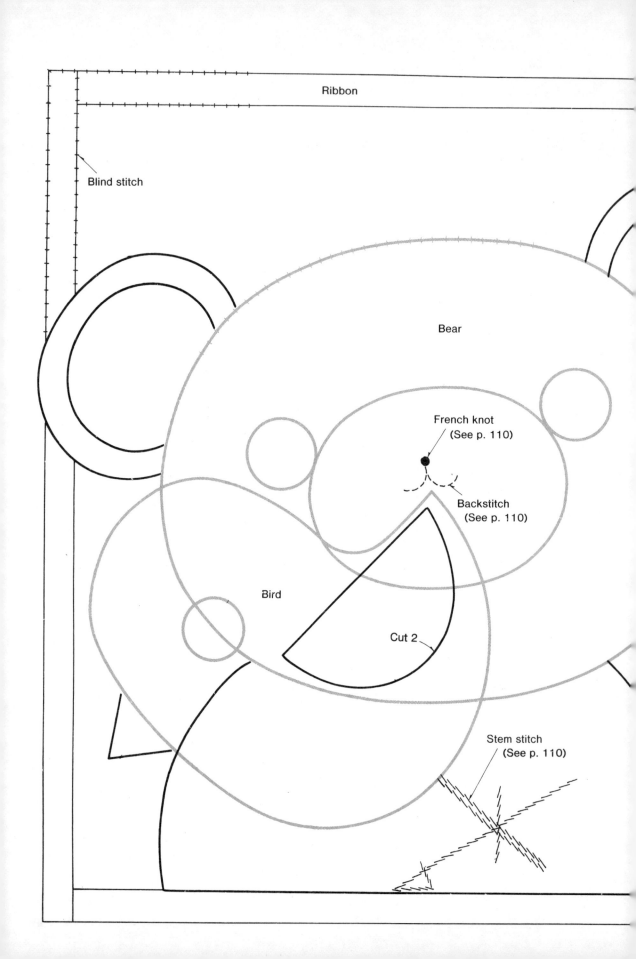

Ribbon

Blind stitch

Bear

French knot
(See p. 110)

Backstitch
(See p. 110)

Bird

Cut 2

Stem stitch
(See p. 110)

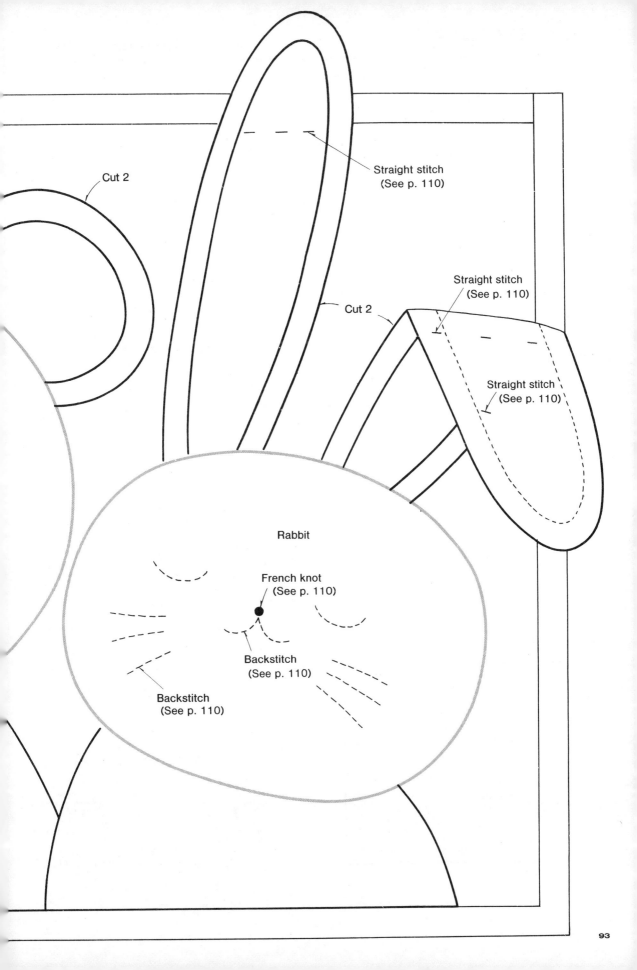

Cut 2

Straight stitch
(See p. 110)

Cut 2

Straight stitch
(See p. 110)

Straight stitch
(See p. 110)

Rabbit

French knot
(See p. 110)

Backstitch
(See p. 110)

Backstitch
(See p. 110)

㊱ BASKET

shown on p. 25

1. Cut one A and two B from white background fabric, no batting.
2. Cut two ruffle pieces from blue background fabric. Cut ribbon in two.

Follow general directions for bassinet assembly, using narrow eyelet only and one 3-in. space in each side for handle.

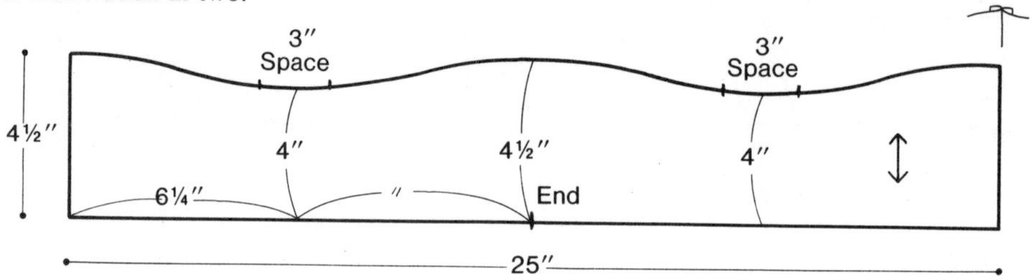

3″ Space
3″ Space
4½″
4″
4½″
4″
6¼″
End
25″

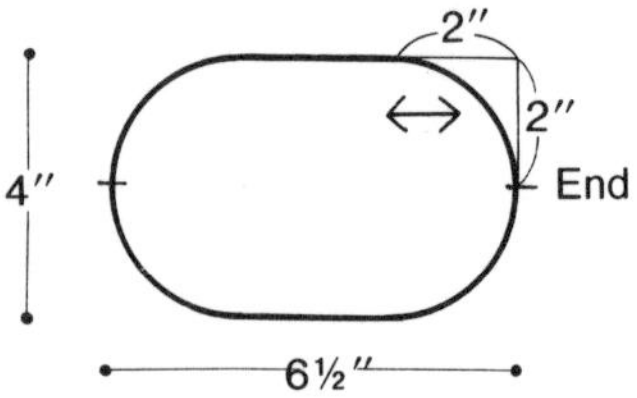

2″
2″
4″
End
6½″

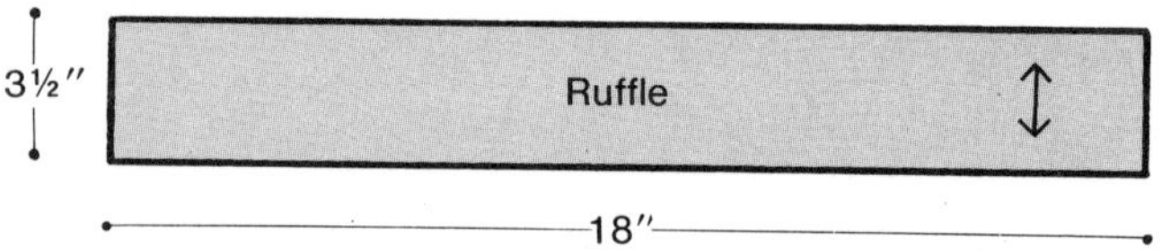

3½″
Ruffle
18″

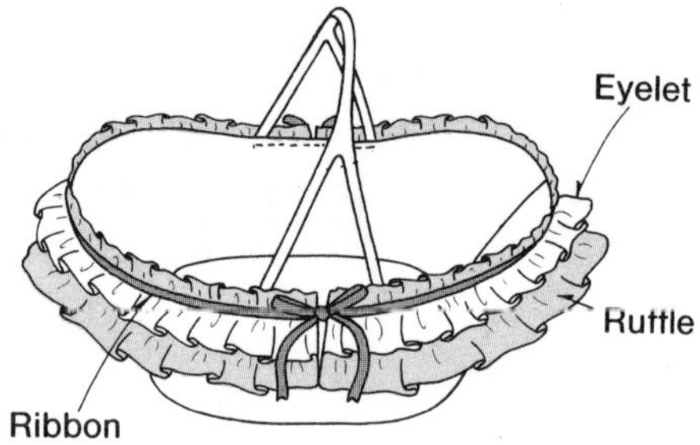

Eyelet
Ruffle
Ribbon

See p. 26 for materials:

㊲ PILLOW,

shown on p. 25

1. Draw patterns full size from scaled diagrams (see p. 107). Add ½-in. seam or hem allowance to all edges of all pieces.
2. Cut two main pieces in blue background fabric. Cut two ruffles in white background fabric.
3. Gather eyelet to 48 ins. and seam ends together.
4. Draw a light line ¾ in. from finished edge (1¼ ins. from raw edge) of one layer of main pillow piece and fit ribbon inside it, Fig. a.
5. Lay gathered eyelet under ribbon and stitch to pillow top, Fig. b.
6. Narrowly hem one edge of ruffle, Fig. c.
7. Gather other edge to fit and lay between fabric layers, seaming all three layers together, leaving small opening for turning, Fig. d.
8. Stuff pillow with filling and slip-stitch, Fig. e.

See p. 26 for materials:

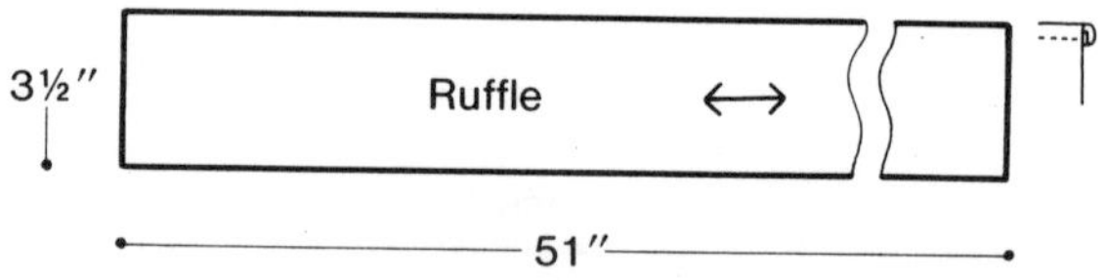

3½″
Ruffle
51″

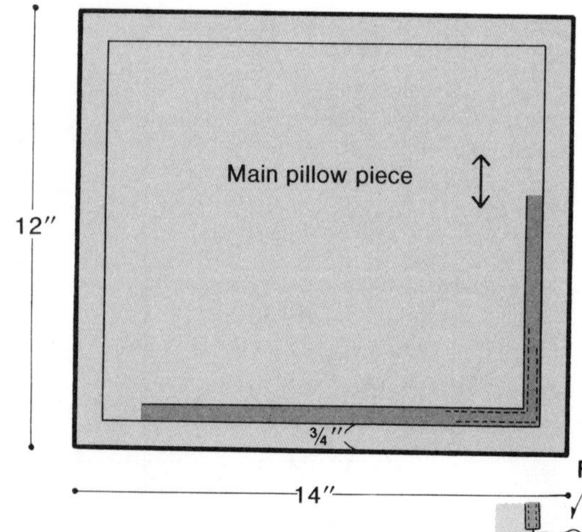

12″
Main pillow piece
¾″
14″

Fig. a

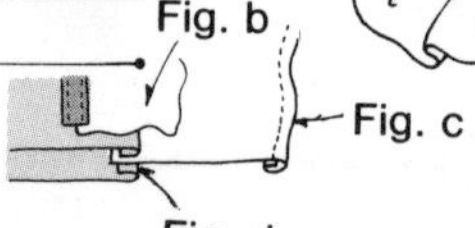

Fig. b
Fig. c
Fig. d

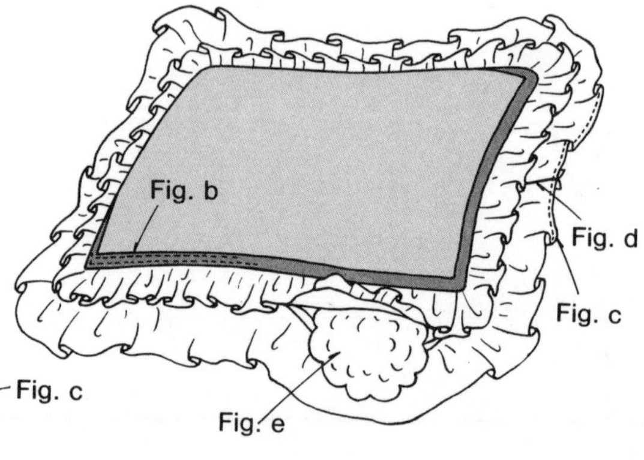

Fig. b
Fig. d
Fig. c
Fig. e

(45) TOY BOTTLE

1. Trace patterns from page 95. Add ¼-in. seam allowance all around.
2. Cut two white from A and two mustard from B.
3. Embroider as shown on one white A piece.

4. Seam A pieces to B pieces.
5. Seam front to back, leaving small opening for turning.
6. Turn right side out, stuff firmly, and slip-stitch opening.

Materials:

Terry cloth	White, 9 ins. sq. Mustard, 5 ins. sq.
Six-strand embroidery floss, less than 1 skein each	Red and black
Polyester fiberfill	Small amount

B

French knots
(See p. 110)

Backstitch
(See p. 110)

A

Straight Stitch
(See p. 110)

MILK

1. Draw patterns full size from scaled diagrams (see p.107). Add ½-in. seam allowance to all edges of all pieces except:

Neck, armhole, and shoulder-strap area.

Lay-on-fold line of back.

2. Cut quilted fabric by pattern layout.

3. Cut eyelet into eight pieces. Gather and stitch to front with bias, as shown, Fig. a.

4. Insert zipper into front, and seam below end of zipper, Fig. b.

5. Seam side and bottom back to front, Fig. c.

6. Press seams open, lay together, and seam across corner to form miter, Fig. d.

7. Bind neck, armhole, and shoulder-strap area, Fig. e.

8. Cut elastic in two, stretch each piece, and stitch at underarm below binding, Fig. f.

9. Sew Velcro® dots on shoulder straps, Fig. g.

10. Sew buttons on outside of straps, Fig. h.

11. Fold and stitch remaining bias binding to make decorative bow for front, Fig. j.

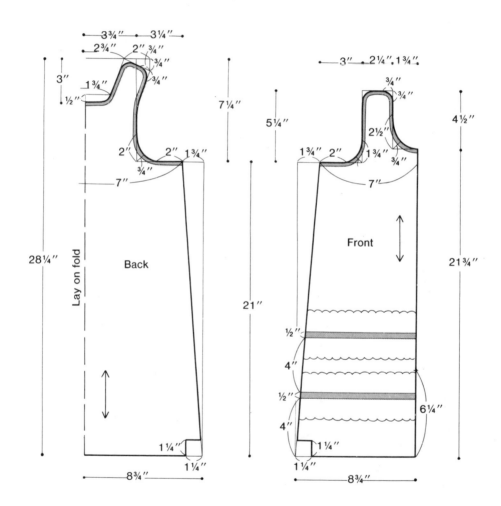

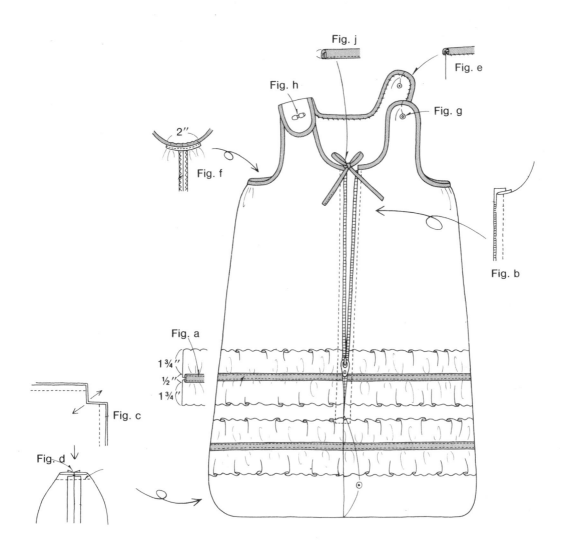

Fig. j

Fig. e

Fig. h

Fig. g

2″

Fig. f

Fig. b

Fig. a

1 ¾″
½″
1 ¾″

Fig. c

Fig. d

Materials:
(Fabrics 36 to 45 ins. wide)

Pink print quilted fabric	⅞ yd.
Pink bias binding (½ in.)	3 yds.
White eyelet edging (1 ½ ins.)	3 yds.
Pink zipper (16 ins.)	1
Velcro® dot	2 pink
Buttons	2
Elastic (¼ in.)	4 ins.

Pattern layout

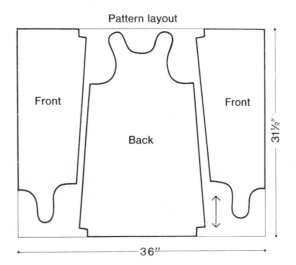

Front

Back

Front

31½″

36″

1. Draw pattern full size from scaled diagrams (see p. 107). Add ¼-in. seam allowance all around.

2. Cut two side pieces and one bottom piece in fabric for each bottle cover.

3. Cut white felt or velour from full-size embroidery diagram. Appliqué and embroider as suggested or with zigzag machine.

4. Gather eyelet to fit edge of felt piece, and stitch both to one side of cover, Fig. a.

5. Seam zipper around curve at top of each side of cover, Fig. b.

6. Seam sides together, Fig. c.

7. Gather straight lower edge and seam to round bottom. Turn cover right side out through zipper.

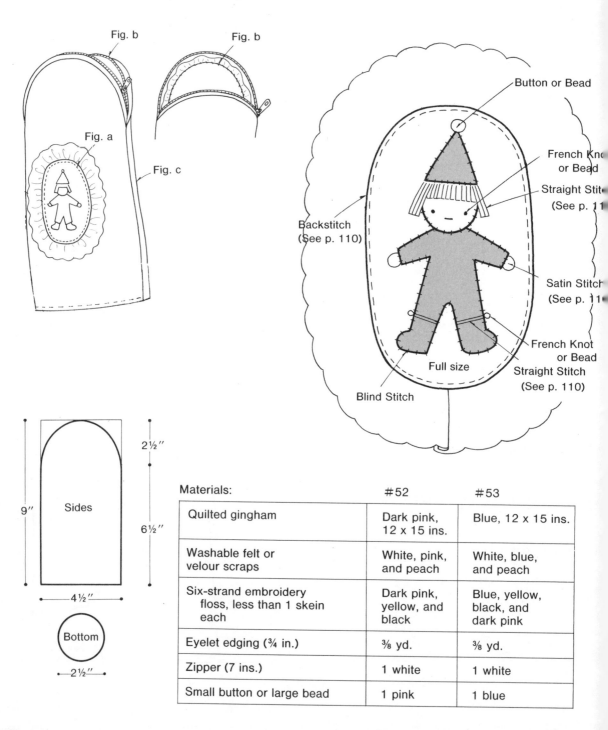

Materials:		#52	#53
Quilted gingham		Dark pink, 12 x 15 ins.	Blue, 12 x 15 ins.
Washable felt or velour scraps		White, pink, and peach	White, blue, and peach
Six-strand embroidery floss, less than 1 skein each		Dark pink, yellow, and black	Blue, yellow, black, and dark pink
Eyelet edging (¾ in.)		⅜ yd.	⅜ yd.
Zipper (7 ins.)		1 white	1 white
Small button or large bead		1 pink	1 blue

(54)(55) COVERALLS shown on p. 44

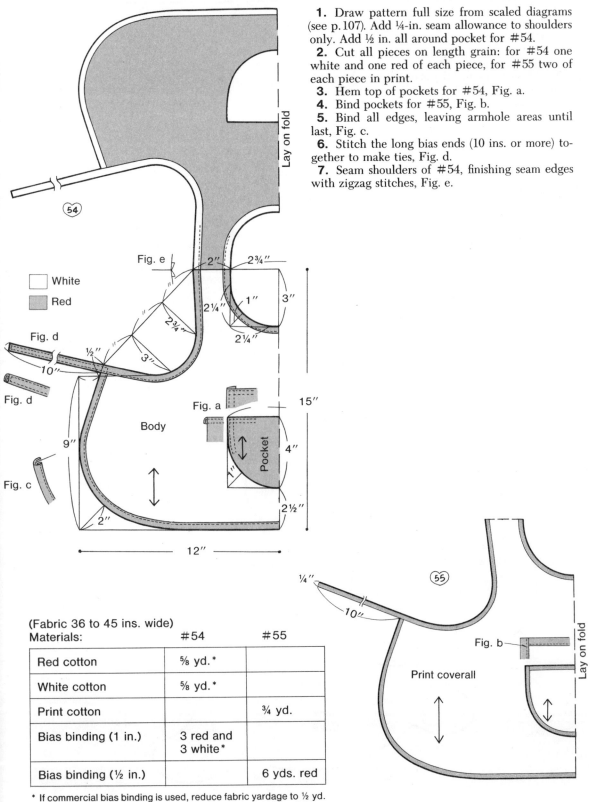

1. Draw pattern full size from scaled diagrams (see p.107). Add ¼-in. seam allowance to shoulders only. Add ½ in. all around pocket for #54.
2. Cut all pieces on length grain: for #54 one white and one red of each piece, for #55 two of each piece in print.
3. Hem top of pockets for #54, Fig. a.
4. Bind pockets for #55, Fig. b.
5. Bind all edges, leaving armhole areas until last, Fig. c.
6. Stitch the long bias ends (10 ins. or more) together to make ties, Fig. d.
7. Seam shoulders of #54, finishing seam edges with zigzag stitches, Fig. e.

White
Red

Body
Pocket
Print coverall

(Fabric 36 to 45 ins. wide)

Materials:	#54	#55
Red cotton	⅝ yd.*	
White cotton	⅝ yd.*	
Print cotton		¾ yd.
Bias binding (1 in.)	3 red and 3 white*	
Bias binding (½ in.)		6 yds. red

* If commercial bias binding is used, reduce fabric yardage to ½ yd. each color. ⅝ yd. allows all binding cut (1½ ins. before folding edges) from leftover fabric.

1. Trace patterns from pages 100–101. Add ⅛-in. seam allowance to all edges of all pieces except:°

Baby's face

2. Cut pieces in quantity marked on each and in colors shown on page 57.

3. Appliqué face on baby, Fig. a.

4. Seam all matching pieces right sides together, turn right side out, and stuff, Fig. b.

5. Gather pompon and stuff, Fig. c.

6. Embroider faces.

7. Join all stuffed pieces with strong hand stitching, Fig. d.

8. Sew bow in place on dog, Fig. e.

° Terry cloth will stretch slightly and may break ordinary straight stitching in seams. It is advisable to use a wide zigzag machine stitch, covering the entire ⅛-in. seam allowance. If working by hand, use an overcast stitch, taking the whole ⅛-in. seam in each stitch, and fastening off firmly at the ends.

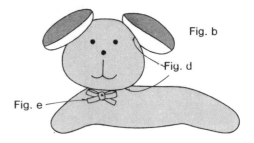

Fig. b

Fig. d

Fig. e

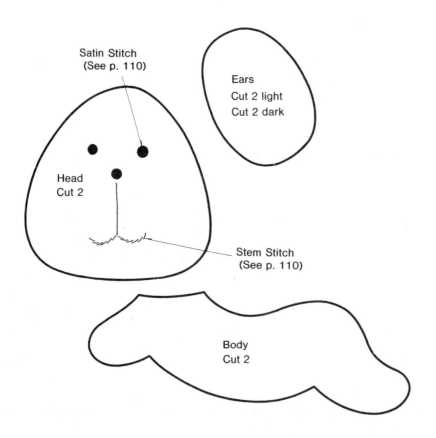

Satin Stitch
(See p. 110)

Ears
Cut 2 light
Cut 2 dark

Head
Cut 2

Stem Stitch
(See p. 110)

Body
Cut 2

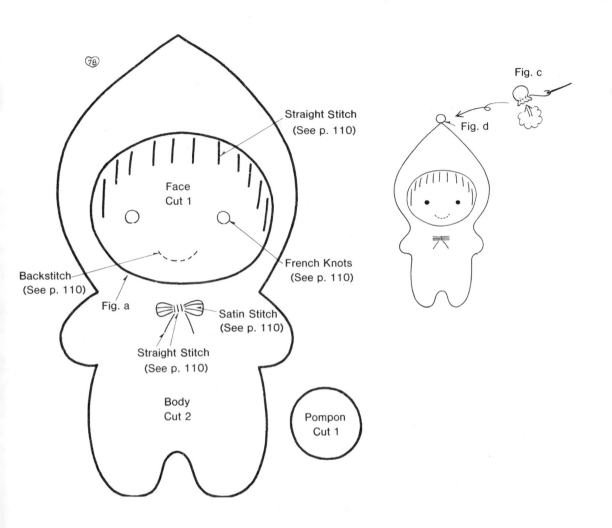

⑦⑧

Straight Stitch
(See p. 110)

Fig. c

Fig. d

Face
Cut 1

French Knots
(See p. 110)

Backstitch
(See p. 110)

Fig. a

Satin Stitch
(See p. 110)

Straight Stitch
(See p. 110)

Body
Cut 2

Pompon
Cut 1

Material:	Baby #77	Baby #78	Dog #79	Dog #80
Terry cloth Cream			6 x 8 ins.	4 x 2 ins.
Yellow			4 x 2 ins.	6 x 8 ins.
White	3 x 3 ins.	3 x 3 ins.	4 x 2 ins.	4 x 2 ins.
Pink	6 x 8 ins.			
Blue		6 x 8 ins.		
Six-strand embroidery floss, less than 1 skein each of tan, yellow, brown, and pink				
Ribbon (¼ in.) ½ yd. blue, ½ yd. red				
Polyester fiberfill, small amount for each				

Continued from page 31

1. Enlarge cloud on page 31 to twice its size.
2. Use all pieces on pages 102–103 full size in colors shown.
3. Use placement shown on page 31. Embroider using stitches suggested or use machine embroidery and appliqué with machine zigzag. Pad clouds with Pellon® Fleece.

Peacock

Yellow

Lavender

Purple

Caramel

Peach

Pink

Yellow

Green

Buttonhole or Zigzag
(See p. 109)

Print

White

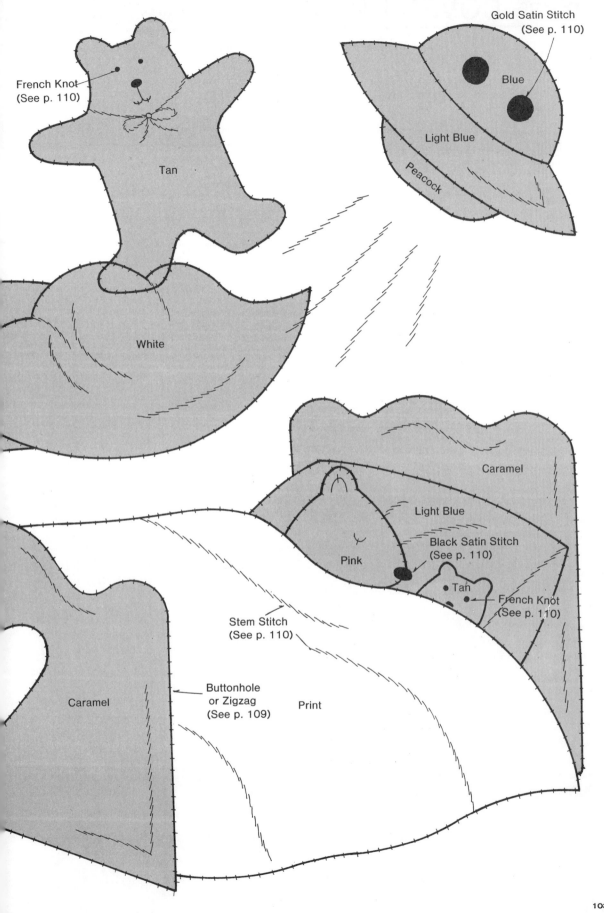

French Knot
(See p. 110)

Gold Satin Stitch
(See p. 110)

Blue

Tan

Light Blue

Peacock

White

Caramel

Light Blue

Black Satin Stitch
(See p. 110)

Pink

Tan

French Knot
(See p. 110)

Stem Stitch
(See p. 110)

Caramel

Buttonhole
or Zigzag
(See p. 109)

Print

1. Trace pattern, extending to length shown. Add ½ in. all around except:
Lay-on-fold edge.
2. Cut back and front of terry.
3. Cut ruffles, 18 ins. of 1½-in. bias, and 1¼ yd. of 2-in. straight of print.
4. Hem pockets, Fig. a.
5. Hem ruffles, Fig. b.
6. Seam shoulders, Fig. c.
7. Sew ruffles to sides, Fig. d.
8. Hem bib edges, Fig. e.°

° All terry edges may be hemmed with zigzag stitching or finished with zigzag and hemmed with straight stitch to avoid thickness of extra fold.

9. Slit back 2 ins. deep. Bind back opening and neck with bias, Fig. f.
10. Make up ties from straight strips and sew to sides, Fig. g.
11. Sew pockets to front, Fig. h.

Materials:	#84
Pink terry	24 x 18 ins.
Print cotton	24 x 24 ins.
Button (½ in.)	1

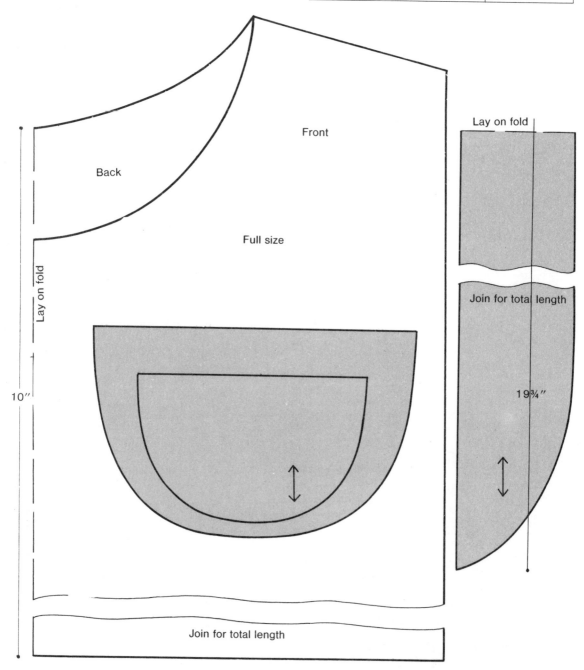

Front

Back

Full size

Lay on fold

10″

Lay on fold

Join for total length

Join for total length

19¾″

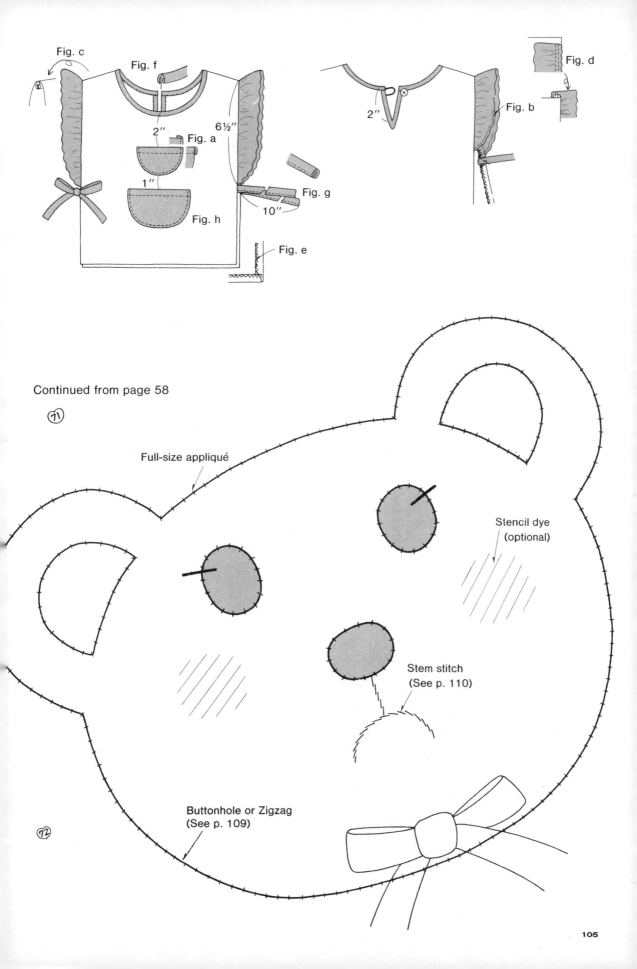

Fig. c

Fig. f

Fig. d

2″

6½″

Fig. a

Fig. b

1″

Fig. h

Fig. g

10″

Fig. e

Continued from page 58

71

Full-size appliqué

Stencil dye
(optional)

Stem stitch
(See p. 110)

72

Buttonhole or Zigzag
(See p. 109)

Continued from page 59

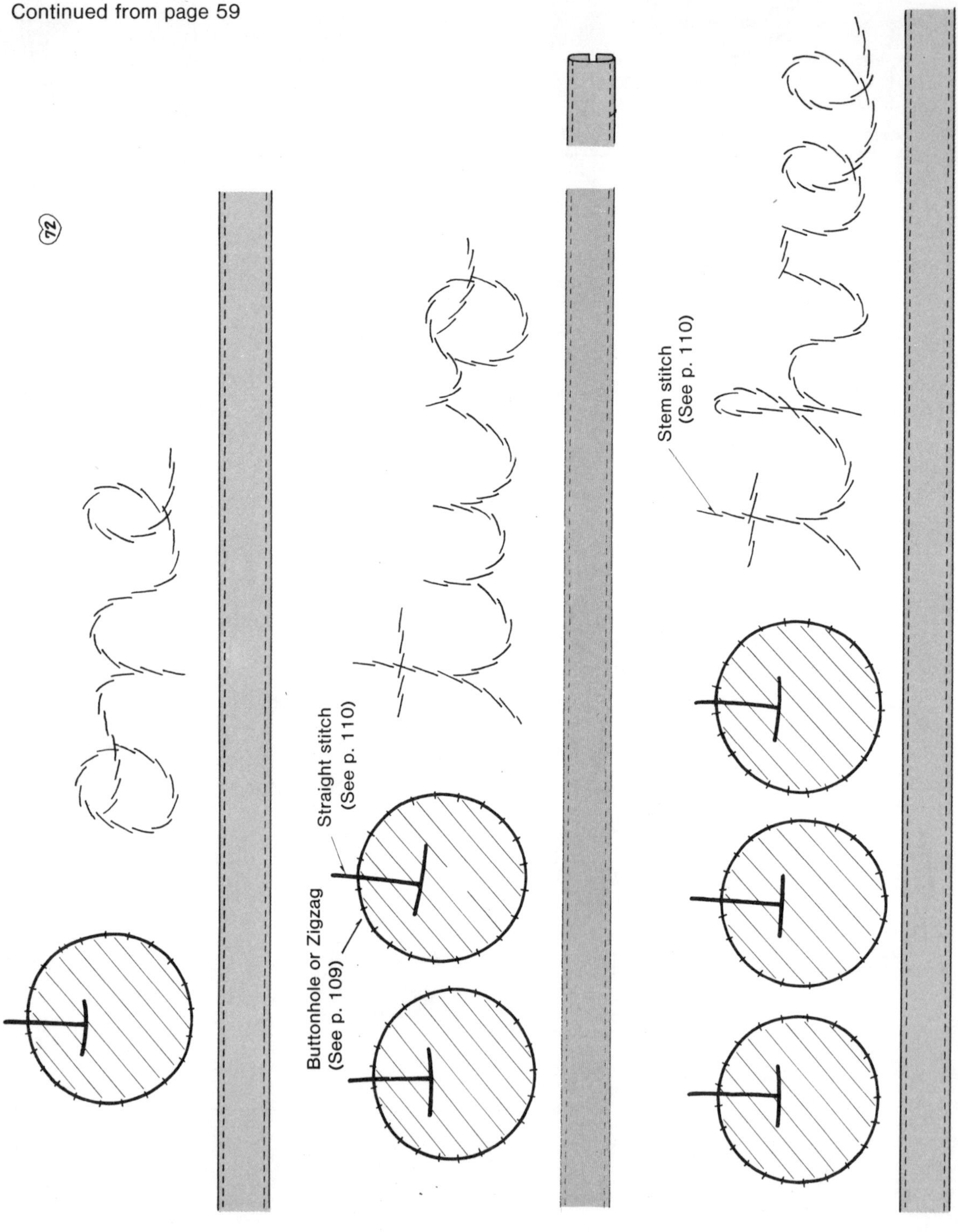

(72)

Buttonhole or Zigzag
(See p. 109)

Straight stitch
(See p. 110)

Stem stitch
(See p. 110)

Enlarging Patterns to Full Size

You will need a large flat drawing surface, a sheet of paper marked into ½-in. graph, and tracing paper. A standard available size of paper is 14 x 17 ins. You may need to put two sheets together for a few patterns. It is difficult to find ½-in. graph, so you may make your own, working over ¼-in. graph for accuracy of line. The only other supplies you'll need are sharp pencils, a good ruler, some type of plastic curve (French or armseye), and an art-gum eraser.

Tape the tracing paper over the graph paper onto the drawing board. Measure the longest straight line—the center back of the panties, for instance—and draw it. Mark the other points, shoulders, waists, etc., from that line, making an obvious dot for each end of each line or curve. Stand back and see if what you've laid out resembles the shape of the garment piece in the book. Using the ruler or the part of the curve that fits the markings, draw the rest of the pattern piece. Add seam allowances and hems as called for.

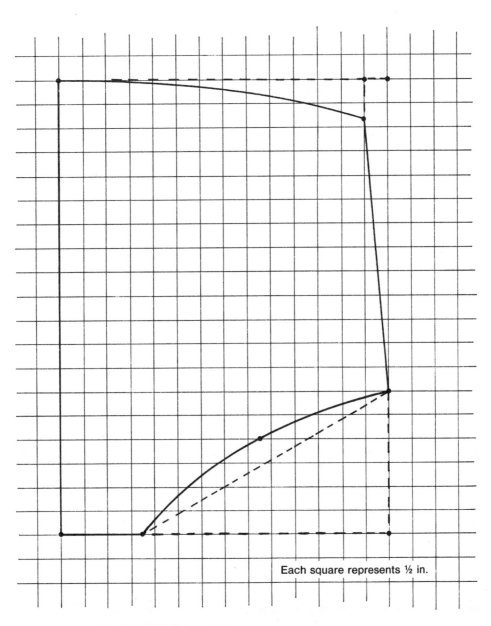

Each square represents ½ in.

Panty pattern from p.10

Cutting and Piecing Bias Binding

Measure along the side and end of a straightened piece of fabric and mark at the same point on each, Fig. a. Draw a line between the two marks; it will be on an exact diagonal to the cross grain and the length grain, Fig. b. Draw as many parallel lines as needed at the desired width of the bias binding—usually about 1½ ins., Fig. c. Cut along these lines. Seam the ends with the right sides together on the straight grain, Fig. d. Press the seams open flat, Fig. e.

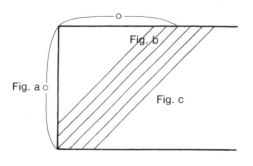

Fig. b

Fig. a

Fig. c

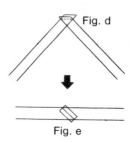

Fig. d

Fig. e

Using Bias Binding

There are three good methods of applying bias binding to a raw fabric edge.

1. The "stitch-in-the-ditch" method makes a clean finish with the machine stitching being almost invisible on the right side. Lay the bias with the right sides together along the edge of the main fabric. Stitch slightly less than one quarter of the distance from the raw edges, Fig. a. Turn the bias over the fabric edge, fold the raw edge of the bias under, press in place so that the folded bias edge covers the seamline. Stitch as close as possible to the bias on the right side of the main fabric, Fig. b, catching the folded edge of the bias on the wrong side, Fig. c.

2. To hand finish on the wrong side, start as for the first method, but stitch an even one quarter of the distance from the edge. Turn the bias over the edge, fold the raw edge under until it meets the line of stitching. Hand finish with an overcast against the stitching, Fig. d.

3. Binding can be finished neatly with machine stitching on the right side. Lay the bias with the right side against the wrong side of the main fabric—raw edges together. Stitch one quarter of the distance from the edge, Fig. e. Turn the bias over the edge, fold the raw edge under, press in place, and machine stitch through the bias and all layers, Fig. f.

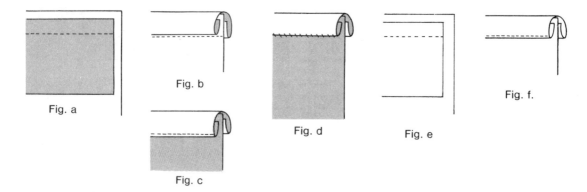

Fig. a

Fig. b

Fig. c

Fig. d

Fig. e

Fig. f.

Finishing the Ends of Bias Binding

When it is necessary to have a smooth, finished end to a bias binding, as on a neck opening, leave an extra ¼ in. extension beyond the main fabric. After seaming the bias to the main fabric, fold the end in, then fold the raw edge of the bias, Fig. g. When the bias edge is folded over and finished, the end will be smooth, Fig. h.

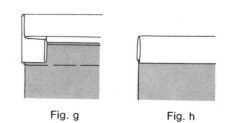

Fig. g

Fig. h

Hems

Turn the fabric to the wrong side to the desired hem width. Fold the raw edge under. Machine stitch near the folded edge, Fig. a. For a finer finish hand overcast the folded edge, Fig. b.

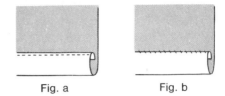

Fig. a   Fig. b

Seams and Seam Finishes

1. The French seam is especially suitable for fine fabrics and infants' clothing. Lay the two pieces of fabric wrong sides together and stitch less than half the width of the seam allowance, Fig. a. Press, then fold back the fabric so that the pieces are right sides together. Seam again just beyond the raw edges, completely encasing the first seam, Fig. b.

2. A flat, felled seam is also completely encased and smooth. Start as for a regular seam with fabric right sides together. Stitch the seam, Fig. c. Trim one edge shorter and turn the other edge over it, Fig. d. Stitch through all layers near the turned edge, Fig. e.

3. Any seam can be stitched right sides together and then finished by one of the following four methods.
   a. Use zigzag machine stitching along raw edges, Fig. f.
   b. Machine stitch through seam edges and trim, Fig. g.
   c. Turn seam edges under and stitch close to turn, Fig. h.
   d. Overcast seam edges by hand, Fig. i.
In none of the above methods do the stitches come through or show on the right side of the garment.

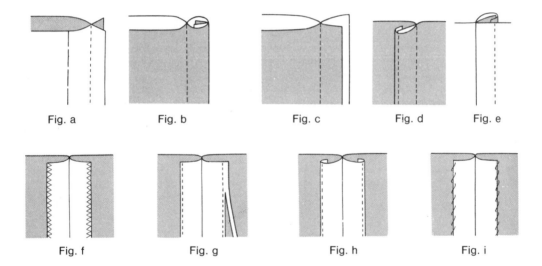

Fig. a   Fig. b   Fig. c   Fig. d   Fig. e

Fig. f   Fig. g   Fig. h   Fig. i

Appliqué

1. Zigzag stitching completely encases the raw edges of any appliqué design so that it is not necessary to turn under the fabric, Fig. a.

2. For traditional hand appliqué, turn and baste the edge of the decorative fabric piece, then attach it to the base fabric with blind stitching, Fig. b.

3. A close buttonhole stitch may be used for appliqué, either with or without turning the fabric edge, depending on the tendency of the fabric to ravel, Fig. c.

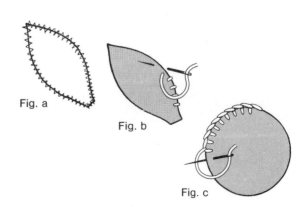

Fig. a

Fig. b

Fig. c

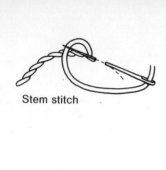

Stem stitch

Running Stitch

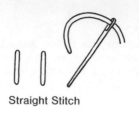

Straight Stitch

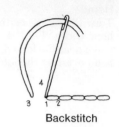

Backstitch

Chain stitch

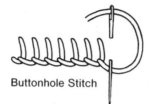

Buttonhole Stitch

Buttonhole Wheel

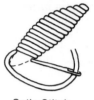

Satin Stitch

Bullion Knot

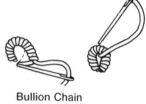

Bullion Chain

Bullion Stitch

Bullion Rose

Fly Stitch

Double Lazy Daisy

Lazy Daisy

Lazy Daisy Flower

French Knot

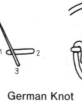

German Knot

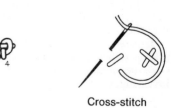

Cross-stitch